Manifesting Violence

Rhetoric + Digitality

MANIFESTING VIOLENCE

White Terrorism, Digital Culture, and the Rhetoric of Replacement

CASEY RYAN KELLY AND WILLIAM JOSEPH SIPE

THE UNIVERSITY OF ALABAMA PRESS
TUSCALOOSA

The University of Alabama Press
Tuscaloosa, Alabama 35487-0380
uapress.ua.edu

Typeface: Minion Pro

Cover image: robodread/stock.adobe.com
Cover design: Sandy Turner Jr.

Cataloging-in-Publication data is available from the Library of Congress.
ISBN: 978-0-8173-2235-9 (cloth)
ISBN: 978-0-8173-6207-2 (paper)
E-ISBN: 978-0-8173-9560-5

To the victims and survivors of mass shootings and white nationalist violence. You are not forgotten.

Contents

Acknowledgments

IT IS DIFFICULT to maintain your mental health and sanity while spending an exorbitant amount of time in the heads of white nationalists and mass murderers. Perhaps such a book is only survivable with the camaraderie of a co-author, someone equally committed to resisting their violent and bankrupt view of the future. Fortunately, we survived with our mental faculties intact (at least we are pretty sure) and have a community of folks to thank for their support and feedback along the way. Casey Kelly would like to first thank his collaborator Will Sipe for all his labor, intellectual contribution, and friendship throughout the completion of this project. It is no small feat to complete a co-authored book while also completing and defending a dissertation, going on job interviews, and then moving across the country all in the same year.

Kelly would also like to thank the Department of Communication Studies at the University of Arkansas (including the helpful feedback of Joe Hatfield, Ryan Neville-Shepard, Meredith Neville-Shepard, and Abe Khan) and the Department of Rhetoric at Wabash College for allowing him to present a version of chapter 4 to faculty and students. Kelly would also like to thank his rhetoric colleagues at the University of Nebraska—Kate Siegfried, Liahnna Stanley, Kristen Hoerl, Justin Kirk, and Aaron Duncan—or their general support of his work. He is also indebted to his father Marvin Kelly, a Vietnam veteran, gun owner, and outspoken critic of gun culture, for his assistance in understanding the mechanics of firearms and the psychology of gun violence. Finally, Kelly wants to thank his spouse, Kristen, for supporting him through this very difficult work.

Will Sipe would like to thank, first and foremost, Casey Kelly for his generosity, intellectual rigor, and guidance throughout a time in Sipe's career summarized by the phrase "suffering from success." Kelly's mentorship and friendship constitute one of the greatest rewards of Sipe's academic journey thus far. Sipe would also like to thank an innumerable group of graduate student peers who shared with him their brilliance, love, and community at the University of Nebraska–Lincoln, including Zoë LaSalle, Jordan Johnson, Katie Kassler, Amanda Brand, and so many others. Sipe would also like to thank faculty members of the honors college at the University of Nevada, Las Vegas, for their care and support during a first semester that abruptly ended in tragedy. Being a witness to a mass shooting brought into stark clarity the importance of this project. Sipe and his students survived, and he continues to heal with the support of those listed above as well as his parents, Todd and Becky Sipe, and his partner in life, Chase Nissen. Thank you for giving him the strength to continue the fight.

Manifesting Violence

Introduction

88 Precepts, 14 Words, 1 Mantra

On Route 65 in northern Arkansas, motorists were once welcomed to the town of Harrison by two billboards.[1] The first featured a stock image of a white family sharing in a fun-loving embrace adjacent to the title message "Welcome to Harrison." Below the sign read "Beautiful Town. Beautiful People. No Wrong Exits. No Bad Neighborhoods." The message evoked a wistful vision of white, small-town America freed from the supposed decay, predation, and criminality of its urban counterpart. Such a greeting conveyed a coded yet familiar colorblind racism that summoned white fear of people of color without explicitly referencing race.[2] Yet, the underlying message is perceptible: Harrison is a white community where people of color are not welcome. This message is also supported by Harrison's legacy as a "sundown town" where lynching and other forms of racist violence forced Black residents to flee at the turn of the twentieth century.[3] The second billboard, however, stated what the first billboard only implies. Directly below, in bold, black print against a yellow backdrop, the accompanying signage read: "'Diversity' is a code word for #whitegenocide." The arresting phrase suggested that the language of progressive multiculturalism (i.e., diversity, equity, and inclusion) is a kind of cipher that conceals secret plots and hidden machinations against the idyllic white family conjured by the first billboard. The message also stokes a perverse curiosity: *how* exactly is something as benign as diversity an existential threat to white people? Who is the mysterious messenger, and how have they come to such knowledge?

To investigate this claim is to look at diversity and antiracism through the looking glass, which is to say that the material reality of structural racism is inverted, upturned, and inside out. But for white onlookers who feel displaced by cultural and economic changes, distressed by policies to combat racial inequality and white privilege, or who feel threatened by immigration and the advancement of people of color, the phrase puts intention behind their inchoate sense of precarity and aggrievement. Most importantly, the slogan is also an invitation down the rabbit hole of online white supremacy. In small print beneath the digital hashtag is the URL fightwhitegenocide.com, a website dedicated to white "human rights" advocacy that calls for "attention to the crime of genocide being committed against the white race."[4] Those who follow the hyperlinks quickly find themselves embedded in an alternative universe of white victimhood, persecution, and paranoia, including links to hundreds of posts, articles, and podcasts intoning the same message: white people are under attack. Fightwhitegenocide.com initiates users into a discourse community in which every advancement of people of color is interpreted as a direct threat to white survival in the twenty-first century. The further one ventures, the more the content grows violent and sinister.

Websites such as these are designed to attract more mainstream white audiences; thus, they downplay overt white supremacy in favor of the language of white pride, nationalism, and cultural preservation.[5] Conserving the purity of white racial stock, they argue, is less about supremacy than about ensuring white survival in a multicultural world.[6] Yet, the slogan advertising this website has a long history connected to white supremacy and ethnonationalism. Indeed, for those familiar with the subculture of white supremacy, they would likely recognize the phrase as a reference to influential segregationist Robert Whitaker's "Mantra," a 221-word racist credo referenced ad nauseum on white supremacist websites, radio shows, and podcasts.[7] "Mantra" was Whitaker's attempt to reframe civil rights and antiracism as surreptitious schemes orchestrated by Jews and people of color to exterminate the white race.[8] Others might also recognize the reference from neo-Nazi David Lane's racist manifesto 88 Precepts and its oft-cited 14 Words: "We must secure the existence of our people and a future for white children."[9] Lane, founder of the white terrorist group the Order, is often credited as one of the originators of the so-called "white genocide" or "great replacement" conspiracy theory in the US The slogan also contains traces from other white supremacist literature, including William Luther Pierce's novel *The Turner Diaries* (1978), Renaud Camus's *The Great Replacement* (2011), and Bat Ye'or's *Eurabia* (2005)—texts that stoke white fears that progressive movements for equality are well-disguised plots to dispossess and replace white Americans and Europeans with immigrants and people of color.[10] Indeed, fightwhitegenocide.com's claim of racial innocence are belied by the slogan's connection to a history of violent white supremacy.

Claims of replacement or "white genocide" might be more easily dismissed as isolated examples of far-right paranoia were it not for a disconcerting spike in hate crimes, racist-motivated mass shootings, and terrorist attacks, along with record high memberships in far-right hate groups across the US[11] Since the election of President Donald Trump in 2016, there has been a resurgence of white nationalism around the globe, fueled in part by the right's embrace of the politics of white grievance and nativism—stances that endeared Trump to the far-right and won the approval of the likes of David Duke and Richard Spencer, along with most Republicans.[12] Included in the coalition of supporters who aided in Trump's victory were groups identifying under the label of the "alt-right," a loose collection of far-right organizations seeking to update and push racist ideas into mainstream politics.[13] Although it is a popular myth that the alt-right was both an organized political entity and instrumental in Trump's election, the amplification of alt-right voices by the press bolstered these groups' legitimacy and aided in their recruitment efforts.[14] In 2017, several of these organizations marched on Charlottesville, Virginia, carrying lit tiki torches to protest the removal of a Confederate statue while chanting "Jews will not replace us" and "you will not replace us!" While some dressed in polo shirts, khakis, and MAGA hats, others donned Ku Klux Klan robes and Nazi uniforms and displayed swastikas and other white supremacist regalia. Proud Boys, Oath Keepers, and Three Percenters carried signs etched with hate group insignias, racist memes, and other symbols traded on white nationalist websites and image boards. While more extreme iterations of racist conspiracy theories were once quarantined to white supremacist book and music stores, the emergent rhetoric of white nationalism provides an aperture into what is now a vast digital network of white supremacy, comprised of websites (Daily Stormer, American Renaissance, Alternative Right), social-networking apps (Gab, Telegram, Parler, WhatsApp), and image boards (Reddit, 4chan, 8chan), where alienated young white men are more easily recruited and radicalized into white supremacy than in the past.

In the digital ecology of white supremacy and nationalism, older racist doctrines once only popular with far-right groups, militias, and neo-Nazi organizations, such as the National Alliance, Ku Klux Klan, Traditionalist Worker Party, the National Socialist White People's Party, and the Order, have been given new life and are now able to reach new audiences.[15] As such, *Manifesting Violence* traces the evolution from analogue white supremacy to digital white nationalism by attending to how new forms, methods of circulation, and modes of rhetorical production help racist ideologies gain wider audiences and accelerate the pace of radicalization toward violence. As Laurie Gries notes, the unique aspects of digital culture permit any image or idea to enter "into new associations, transformations, and generates a multiplicity of consequences."[16] As a consequence of digital circulation, racist ideologies are remixed, recomposed, and recontextualized to give them new relevance. Thus, we illustrate how white supremacist ideologies are recrafted in and through forms of participatory media, in which engagement between users is anonymous, playful, and memetic. Since it is nearly impossible to generalize about all forms of racism that live comfortably in far-right digital ecologies, we argue that the rhetoric of replacement offers an opening into the kind of racist rhetoric promulgated online that has motivated users to commit acts of terrorism. In fact, the digital rhetoric of racial replacement has played a vital role in acclimating the uninitiated to more extreme racist principles. For example, the mass murderer who killed ten and injured three Black persons in Buffalo, New York, claimed that he casually stumbled upon white genocide discourse while browsing Reddit and quickly become radicalized and committed to violence on the more extremist imageboard 4chan/pol/. The same can be said for other mass murders who found the rhetoric of racial replacement on white nationalist websites, encrypted messaging apps, and imageboards.

We anchor our study in the Great Replacement myth because it is able to circulate in extremist digital networks and migrate onto more mainstream media news sources. The rhetoric of replacement exists in both worlds because it begins with a seemingly innocuous plea to protect and appreciate white people as part of a multicultural future but ultimately ends with a call to arms to do whatever it takes to "secure the existence of our people and a future for white children." It is, therefore, no coincidence that these digital communities have radicalized a new generation of white terrorists, whose manifestos and online screeds are littered with references to racial replacement. Although their radicalization was completed online, white terrorists did not begin their journey on extremist platforms. Rather, their radicalization began when a trusted news source or someone on an entertainment imageboard suggested that their feelings of alienation and victimhood were not an accident but by design. In the perpetrators' own words, the rhetoric of replacement incited them to make the leap from word to deed. They accumulated arsenals of military-grade weaponry and massacred large groups of unsuspecting people, children included, while they were buying groceries, running errands, or visiting their place of worship. Massacres at Oslo, Charleston, Christchurch, El Paso. Pittsburgh, Gilroy, Buffalo, Bratislava, and Allen—all of this violence was aided by the fact that in far-right digital ecosystems, violence is a form of entertainment and empowerment. For instance, the Christchurch gunman live-streamed his attack in the style of a first-person shooter video game and jokingly encouraged his audience to subscribe to gamer celebrity PewDiePie. This growing list of cities terrorized by white supremacists evince not just a national epidemic of gun violence but an accelerating pattern of white radicalization that has lowered the threshold between racist beliefs and racist violence. Even more alarming is that the great replacement theory now has a mainstream voice among influential pundits such as Laura Ingraham and Tucker Carlson, who routinely reference the theory on their nightly broadcasts. With increasing white paranoia about the impending demographic shift toward a nonwhite majority by 2045, the probability of future white supremacist violence demands immediate attention.

This book examines how the rhetoric of replacement that occurs in far-right digital ecologies radicalizes and prepares audiences for white supremacist violence. We analyze the writings of white supremacist terrorists, tracing the rhetorical influences of digital white supremacy and nationalism in their manifestos, to explain how the rhetoric of white genocide has proven fundamental in compelling a leap from talk to violence. From our reading of these manifestos, we advance three central arguments. First, we argue that the rhetoric of replacement reframes white terrorism as an empowering form of *defensive* violence, necessary to ensure white survival in a multicultural future. By coopting the language of multiculturalism and antiracism, the promulgators of the great replacement theory construct a precarious form of whiteness that must be secured against the threat of racial difference. Second, as the by-products of digital culture, we argue that the manifestos are *memetic* insofar as they encourage others to imitate, copy, and replicate acts of symbolic and physical violence. Like memes, these manifestos act as conduits for the transmission of white nationalist ideas and practices so that they can self-replicate, mutate, and evolve within digital enclaves that are largely insulated from antiracist activism. Third, the process of radicalization is facilitated by the playful, transgressive, and ironic engagement that characterizes a great deal of anonymous digital communication. That is to say, it is often difficult for users to tell the difference between earnest expressions of white supremacy from dedicated adherents and shocking humor meant to signal a user's "creative" use of irreverence (so-called "lulz") to disavow a more than sincere set of racist commitments. Either way, we argue, the unstable meaning of racist "jokes" in digital ecosystems normalizes white supremacy and de-emphasizes its violent consequences. Thus, at both a formal and ideational level, the patterned repetition of white supremacist content that appears in manifestos not only reflects the rhetorical norms and practices found in far-right digital ecologies but also aids in the transmission of racist tropes so that they can spread quickly, survive, and adapt through acts of imitation. As rhetoric scholars, we seek to analyze white terrorist manifestos and their intertextual fragments closely in order to make sense of how particular forms of symbolic action authorize white supremacist violence and invite others to imitate it. We offer this book as an intervention that provides insights into the relationship between the digital rhetoric of replacement and the violence it engenders.

FROM "RACE SUICIDE" TO "WHITE GENOCIDE"?

The rhetoric of replacement, or white genocide, represents an evolution of white supremacist discourse that begins in the late nineteenth century as racist population science (eugenics and demography) and, over a century later, transforms into conspiracy theories expressed through racist memes and manifestos. Although this book focuses on its digital manifestations, it is important to note how theories of replacement have evolved as white supremacy has been continually reshaped by historical events and the racial politics in the US. Thus, what begins as a rhetoric of "race suicide" transforms into a digital conspiracy theory of "white genocide."

In the US, the term "race suicide" first emerged from the late nineteenth-century and early twentieth-century eugenics movement. Influenced by sociologist Edward A. Ross's address entitled "The Cause of Racial Superiority," some prominent scientists and political leaders expressed grave concern that higher rates of non-white immigration and white women's economic advancement would precipitate the demographic decline of white birth rates.[17] For instance, in *Winning the West*, President Theodore Roosevelt ruminated over the "the warfare of the cradle," an aphorism suggesting that immigrants and people of color would forcefully displace and subsequently subjugate white Americans.[18] Racist tomes, such as Madison Grant's *The Passing of the Great Race* (1916) and Lothrop Stoddard's *The Rising Tide of Color Against White World-Supremacy* (1920), warned of "race suicide" as a consequence of declining white fertility rates and the mongrelization of white racial stock through miscegenation.[19] Grant argued that the nation's greatness was owed to the innate superiority of Nordic bloodlines and warned that immigration from Southern and Eastern Europe—not to mention Asia, Latin America, and Africa—would pollute the nation's gene pool. Despite lacking scientific rigor, Grant's ideas were praised by both President Warren G. Harding and President Calvin Coolidge and influenced the Congressional architects of the 1924 Immigration Act.[20] Grant's work also received high praise from Adolf Hitler, who called *The Passing of the Great Race* his "Bible."

In part, the popular reception of eugenics was owed to centuries of colonialist, white supremacist, and pro-slavery discourse, which had already cultivated fear that interracial sexual intercourse would dilute the purity of whiteness and disrupt the economic system and legal categorization schemas of race that had theretofore guaranteed structural white supremacy. To be sure, racial supremacy was not an entirely an invention of slaveholders and the Confederacy. Grant and other eugenicists were upper-class Northeasterners who shared a xenophobic reaction to new populations of immigrants from Eastern and Southern Europe. The expansion of American empire to places such as the Philippines, Puerto Rico, and Hawaii raised concerns among the white Northern elite that the nation would no longer remain a white republic. Their pseudoscientific theories of racial degeneracy were similar to other forms of racist thought that were used in previous decades to legitimize indigenous genocide and exclude indigenous, Latinx, Asian, and Black people from the privileges of citizenship and personhood.

Not contained solely within the US South, anti-miscegenation discourse, along with the one-drop rule of hypodescent, was premised on the more general belief that mixing white and Black blood would result in the dilution of whiteness and the waning of the Nordic bootstrapping spirit. Like Southern slaveholders, Northern eugenicists believed that miscegenation was an existential threat to white people. As Jared Sexton observes, "The obsession of white supremacist discourse with interracial sexuality quickly slides into paranoia about the pollution of the white racial stock, a process resulting in a universal 'mongrelization' tantamount to genocide of the white population."[21] In the early twentieth century, the unique confluence of racist population science, institutionalized demography, and the late importation of Thomas Malthus's 1798 *Essay on the Principle of Population* into the United States scientific community lent authoritative support to xenophobic, nativist, and white supremacist movements, which promoted the notion that the mere existence of immigrant and communities of color in the US threatened whiteness with extinction.[22]

It is perhaps ironic that Nazism, which had wholeheartedly embraced American theories of race suicide, was later defeated by the same nation from which those ideas had germinated. Though the phrase temporarily disappearing from public life during World War II, race suicide reemerged in the postwar period, but this time it was articulated as part of a well-orchestrated Jewish conspiracy to dispossess and subjugate the white race. During the era of desegregation and Civil Rights activism, white supremacist organizations not only preached doctrines of racial supremacy but also characterized nearly any demographic or economic advancement of people of color as an intentional and premeditated attack on white Western culture.

Replacing race suicide, the phrase white genocide first appeared in a 1972 issue of *White Power*, the official newspaper of the American Nazi Party (later renamed the National Socialist White People's Party), as a subversive plot to replace white people altogether. One essay argued that the widespread availability of birth control had, by design, suppressed fertility rates in developed majority white nations to the advantage of lesser-developed nations. The intention of promulgating birth control, the authors feared, was the demographic extinction of the white race. Another essay in the issue declared that "Busing is genocide!" and argued that desegregation was a deliberate attempt by "race mixers" to destroy white culture.[23] In an op-ed, publisher Matt Koehl surmised that "today our race is engaged in a life-and-death struggle for survival on this continent. It is threatened with genocide. The prospect of our people gradually dying out and becoming a subservient minority race by the next century is inevitable *unless* the current genocidal drift is halted."[24] As we argue throughout this book, the adoption of the term genocide to characterize demographic transformations profoundly changed white supremacist discourse by amplifying the urgency for immediate action to save the white race. The word genocide, first coined by Polish lawyer Raphäel Lemkin in 1944 (from the Greek prefix *genos,* or race, and the Latin suffix *cide,* or to kill), was adopted by the international community after World War II in the wake of the Holocaust as a term that named the systematic murder and cultural destruction of a people, race, or ethnicity.[25]

Whereas *suicide* implied that a white demographic decline was a self-inflicted injury, *genocide* suggested declining birth rates were the result of a concerted and systematic effort to exterminate white people. Naming motives in such stark terms reframed the cause of white supremacy, including the possibility of violence, as a defensive and reasonable response to systematic racial persecution. This new phrase constructed a powerful, racist enemy with the will to engage in collective mass violence. To quote Kenneth Burke, naming motives "prepare us for some functions and against others, for or against the persons representing these functions."[26] Claims of white genocide rhetorically inverted the power dynamics between white people and people of color, disavowing the historic destruction, subjugation, and exclusion of minoritized populations. The term also placed intention and malice behind social and economic changes, offering a grid of intelligibility through which white people might read the presence of difference as a threat to their existence, ranging from policy controversies over busing, voting rights, and affirmative action programs to the increasing visibility and upward mobility of immigrants and people of color.

A decade later, David Lane's manifesto 88 Precepts transformed white genocide into the rallying cry of the contemporary white supremacist movement, often compressed into a 14 Words slogan. Although deeply invested in white supremacy and the establishment of a white ethnostate, Lane's text emphasized white vulnerability and victimization at the hands of "race mixers" and "race traitors," a faceless group of elites with significant power in government, finance, and the media. He did not explicitly name Jews as the culprits; however, his claims bear the markers of anti-Semitic banking and media conspiracy theories that trace their lineage to the *Protocols of the Learned Elders of Zion* (1903).[27] What was novel about his approach was his preoccupation with the protection of white children. Now loudly echoed in contemporary manifestos, the far right's compulsive reiteration of Lane's 14 Words brushes whiteness with a patina of innocence and vulnerability to build the case for defensive violence.[28]

In summarizing Lane's influence, Alexander Laban Hinton argues that "it is at this time that the white power movement increasingly adopts discourse of white victimization and the idea emerges that whites have the right to forcefully and even violently respond to the threat of what begins to be called 'white genocide.'"[29] Thus, Lane's shift in emphasis recasts theories of race suicide and fears of miscegenation in more malicious and conspiratorial terms. Lane explained that "People who allow others not of their race to live among them will perish, because the inevitable result of a racial integration is racial interbreeding which destroys the characteristics and existence of a race. Forced integration is deliberate and malicious genocide, particularly for a People like the White race, who are now a small minority in the world."[30] As this passage illustrates, Lane's manifesto inverted the power dynamics of structural racism in order to disavow the continuity of white racial hegemony into the late twentieth century. In Lane's framing of white people as an aggrieved minority, there was a greater urgency and clearer justification for violence.

Although Lane was the head of a terrorist organization, some of his beliefs were not beyond the pale of more mainstream conservative politics. As Paul E. Johnson observes, the shift in the rhetoric of conservative populism that wrought the election of Ronald Reagan was fueled, in part, by a white backlash against Civil Rights activism and a growing perception on the right that whites were the victims of social and institutional discrimination (robust taxation, affirmative action programs, anti-discrimination laws, etc.).[31] The Reagan Revolution, too, was underwritten by white fears that the demographic makeup of the country was changing and that the structural privileges whites once enjoyed would be lost to the mandates of a parasitic welfare state and the dictates of progressive multiculturalism. During this period, the difference between the mainstream white backlash and militant white supremacy was a matter of degree, rather than kind.

Throughout the 1990s, white supremacist organizations capitalized on antigovernment sentiment following the botched federal sieges at Ruby Ridge and the Branch Davidian compound in Waco, Texas, and the subsequent rallying cry of Timothy McVeigh and the *Turner Diaries*–influenced bombing of the Oklahoma City Alfred P. Murrah Federal Building in 1995.[32] While militia and hate-group membership increased during this period, white supremacist organization were largely clandestine and faced challenges in recruiting new members.[33] Prior to the emergence of the internet, even as their rhetoric evolved, white supremacist organizations faced difficulty recruiting new members outside of neo-Nazi bookstores, rock concerts, bars, motorcycle clubs, and prison gangs.[34] Whether it was the shaved heads, tattoos, and leather jackets of neo-Nazis or the paramilitary look of right-wing militias, white power extremists crafted an alienating aesthetic that tended to repel most outsiders even those harboring racist sentiments.[35] Before the rise of digital media, white supremacist subcultures were mostly solemn, overtly violent, and rigidly hierarchal—demanding obedience and serious commitment from their members. Their racist doctrines were too extreme and violently transgressive to appeal to most moderate conservatives. In the post-Civil Rights era, white supremacists largely operated in secret, and their public sympathizers adopted coded dog whistles to disguise their racist beliefs.[36]

Although white supremacy never disappeared, the confluence of white political aggrievement and new digital technologies have contributed to the recent resurgence in hate group membership and the mainstreaming of racist rhetoric. The election of Barack Obama, the nation's first Black president, in 2008 energized a white conservative backlash that characterized the President's agenda as reverse racism and promulgated racist conspiracy theories that Obama was not a US citizen.[37] In highlighting Obama's eight years in power as a sign of waning white power, Donald Trump secured victory in the 2016 election by running on a platform of anti-immigration, antiglobalization, and the politics of white victimhood. As Bradley A. Serber points out, Trump's most significant contribution to the rhetoric of white supremacy was to supplant the dog-whistle racism of the Obama years with "howling," or a more explicit though plausibly deniable form of racist discourse that "undermines the integrity of the political system and opens the way for more violent and authoritarian methods of domination based on the suppression and exclusion of an identified and dehumanized 'Other.'"[38]

Although hate group membership and hate crimes surged after Trump's election—evidenced by the violent Unite the Right rally at Charlottesville in 2017—the renaissance in white supremacy is owed to the growth and accessibility of digital technologies, which enabled far-right groups to recruit virtually and anonymously in new online networks.[39] members of the so-called alt-right did not spontaneously emerge to crown Trump their savior in 2016, but, as some of the internet's earliest adopters, had been organizing in digital spaces over the previous decade.[40]

A loose collection of mischief-seeking and irreverent internet dwellers, the alt-right diverged from paleoconservatives and libertarians but also from self-serious white nationalists in their use of transgressive and offensive humor, trolling, and tech savvy to repudiate the politically correct norms of civic discourse.[41] In one sense, new digital networks, composed of imageboards (Reddit, 4chan), microblogging cites (Gab), social-network applications (X, formerly Twitter, Facebook, Truth Social, Parler), and encrypted messaging applications (Telegram, WhatsApp), afforded new connections between disparate far-right communities. But in another sense the alt-right attracted new and unlikely supporters by embracing the playpen ethos of devoted internet users, which often entailed the quasi-ironic exchange of offensive content and racist humor.[42]

For those raised in so-called "internet culture," the assumption that shocking and vile content is just for the lulz (shorthand for laughter at someone's else expense) and that only naïve "normies" (internet outsiders) would take such claims seriously has made it extraordinarily difficult to discern the difference between ironic jokes and deadly serious racism. Ultimately, the difference is irrelevant, given that the outcome is the same: users and audiences learn to dissociate between irreverent humor and straightforward violent racism. Neo-Nazis and white nationalists have exploited this ambiguity to normalize white supremacy, while also sabotaging outsiders by convincing them their communications are "just jokes" and "just the internet," where nothing really matters and everything is entertainment. For some, digital white supremacy offer a sense of community in common style of irreverent humor, or even race and/or gender affinity. Yet entertainment and community are entrée to more extreme and violent content, e.g., anti-Semitic conspiracy theories, violent Islamophobia, ethnonationalism, eugenics and racist population science, Holocaust denial, pro-Hitler memes, genocide propaganda, violent pornography, images of death and gore, and other extreme forms of extremist discourse. Users might encounter other esoteric right-wing doctrines, such as ecofascism, the Dark Enlightenment, and accelerationism, all ideologies that seek to hasten the collapse of democracy through armed violence.[43] Lulz is a lure that brings new audiences looking for amusement and community into a vast world of deadly serious white supremacy.

Lulz aside, the alt-right's ultimate goal is to normalize white supremacy, meaning that jokes and amusement were simply one means by which racist talking points might be seen as acceptable to express and debate in public. Alt-right conspiracy theories are able to spread virally, often through a rebuke of "political correctness," to eventually make their way in more reputable conservative news sources. Although this book focuses on the words of white terrorists, the rhetoric of replacement now appears in more mainstream conservative media outlets and has been openly embraced by some elected officials and candidates for office. Most notably, in April 2021 Tucker Carlson asserted during his nightly *Fox News* program that "the Democratic Party is trying to replace the current electorate, the voters now casting ballots, with new people, more obedient voters from the third world. But they become hysterical because that's what's happening actually." Similarly Laura Ingraham told her viewers that Democrats "want to replace you, the American voter, with newly amnestied citizens and an ever-increasing number of chain migrants."[44] When the Anti-Defamation League called for Carlson to be fired for his comments, Rep. Matt Gaetz (R-Florida) tweeted that Carlson was "CORRECT about Replacement Theory as he explains what is happening to America," and called the ADL a "racist organization."[45]

Other conservative politicians have embraced the more overtly racist overtones of replacement rhetoric. In 2017, Rep. Steve King (R-Iowa) tweeted, "We can't restore our civilization with somebody else's babies."[46] When asked to explain his tweet, he replied "You've got to keep your birth rate up, and that you need to teach your children your values . . . In doing so, you can grow your population, you can strengthen your culture, and you can strengthen your way of life."[47] In 2021, Rep. Elise Stefanik (R-New York) ran a Facebook ad that claimed that "Radical Democrats are planning their most aggressive move yet: a PERMANENT ELECTION INSURRECTION. Their plan to grant amnesty to 11 MILLION illegal immigrants will overthrow our current electorate and create a permanent liberal majority in Washington."[48] Although conservative politicians and media personalities tend to avoid overt advocacy of white supremacy, the racial politics of these statements could not be more clear: white political power is waning, white culture is under attack by non-white foreigners, and the political left is fomenting a dangerous demographic shift that will permanently disenfranchise white people.

The language and vectors of white supremacy have evolved from the early twentieth to the twenty-first century; however, it is important to keep in mind that the ideology's ultimate function and purpose remains to preserve essential biological differences and racial hierarchies that protect white social, economic, and institutional power against the threat of progressive social change. Dylan Rodriguez uses the term "white reconstruction" to characterize this persistent refabrication of "new modalities of white self-vindication," marked by a "*logic* of reform, rearticulation, adaption, and revitalization that shapes white social and ontological self-and-world-making within the aspiration, present-tense and violently future-oriented projects of Civilization/Manifest Destiny/Progress."[49] The rhetoric of replacement is deployed as a warrant for the reconstitution of white sovereignty,[50] or the authority to rule the polity in the name of the white citizenry—the apotheosis of which is found in the restorationist fantasy of a solely white ethnostate.[51] Fears of demographic shifts amplify paranoia that in the future white people will be deprived of the capacity to make decisions in the name of "the people." But, as Eric King Watts observes, the facts of the matter are ancillary insofar as the purpose of racist conspiracy theories is to prepare aggrieved white adherents for "tribal warfare" and cycles of militarization against "blackened biothreats," ranging from fears of Black Lives Matter and immigrant caravans invading the suburbs to teaching Critical Race Theory in public schools and gender-affirming health care.[52] As an "imagined community,"[53] the the concept of the white ethnostate grounds its claim to sovereignty in enmity: the Other's existence is a mortal biophysical threat to "our" own. In Achilles Mbembe way of characterizing it, this form of necropolitical "sovereignty consists of the will and the capacity to kill so as to live."[54] The threshold to killing in the name of white sovereignty is lowered not only by the enemy's hostility toward white people but also by the detached and dehumanizing language used to describe their enemies: they are vermin, rats, snakes, and cockroaches who infest, invade, flood, spill, swarm, and overrun.[55] Their innate capacity for sexual reproduction prefigures their bodies as weapons—their very survival is a threat to white civilization. In this schema of self-defense, white lives register more "emphatically as lives" than immigrants and persons of color.[56] "Those people" come from "shithole countries" with the intention of robbing hard-working, white Americans of their racial entitlements and of putrefying their blessed shores.[57] Simply put, the purpose of such rhetoric is to prepare its adherents for violence and martyrdom in the name of a white future.

THE FAR-RIGHT DIGITAL ECOSPHERE

In mainstream conservative media, references to replacement theory offer more sanitized versions of the racist talking points that appear on white nationalist websites.[58] Although one or two degrees removed from the virulent original sources, these scattered references to replacement theory point to a symbiotic relationship between the far-right digital ecosphere and mainstream conservative figures who enable white supremacist ideas to gain a national audience. For instance, leaked emails showed that Stephen Miller, former Trump adviser and architect of the administration's Muslim immigration ban, was directly influenced by content from Vdare.com, a white nationalist website that traffics in white genocide discourse.[59] Trump himself retweeted a story alleging that white farmers in South Africa were being systematically murdered and dispossessed as part of post-apartheid land reform. The story, which has since been debunked, made its way to the President's Twitter feed through the aggressive campaigning of far-right bloggers, podcasters, and influencers, such as Simon Roche, Stefan Molyneux, and Mike Cernovich, to get the attention of mainstream conservative figures and journalists.[60] By the time the story was discredited, the damage had already been done. Ultimately, one of the alt-right's main goals is to push white nationalist ideas into the so-called "Overton window," a name for the range of acceptable ideas and policies that can be legitimately advocated by political stakeholders.[61] The Overton window is not immovable. It can expand, contract, or slide across the political spectrum depending on the evolution of social norms and values. The goal of white nationalists is to extend the window further to the right by normalizing their ideas and making them acceptable to discuss in public. The appearance of white genocide discourse outside of far-right books, forums, and websites indicates both the scope of white supremacist influence within conservative media culture and also the extent to which white supremacist ideas have been successfully repackaged as respectable, or at the very least debatable, political beliefs. Most importantly, white nationalists leverage their influence with conservative journalists and politicians to reach new audiences and direct traffic to their websites.

We contend that white terrorism, along with its twisted, vile prose, is an outgrowth of this confluence between conservative media and far-right digital networks. Far-right influencers and content creators aggressively cycle racist content on digital sites and image boards—memes, diatribes, clickbait articles, and links to white nationalist organizations—which can subsequently be distilled or diluted into less conspicuously violent, extremist messages. These messages can be promoted and circulated throughout popular social media platforms and, in some cases, can even capture the attention of conservative journalists and politicians. These more sanitized messages reach broader audiences and direct them to websites and forums that initiate and acclimate new adherents to white supremacy. Fragments of white genocide in conservative media culture thus serve as a gateway to everyday white supremacy, "where people can be radicalized toward far-right ideologies and actions."[62] Fox News, Newsmax, and One America News Network, and Sinclair Broadcasting Group are adjacent but interrelated *ecosystems* that help facilitate the mainstreaming of extreme far-right content.

At the same, we are mindful that the circulation of racial replacement rhetoric is not the product of conservative and far-right media alone. After all, many of us have friends or relatives in our extended social networks who have unwittingly shared disinformation or white supremacist content. To our own shock, some of us have accidentally done it ourselves. Whitney Phillips and Ryan M. Milner point out that the mainstream and left-of-center press played their part as well, amplifying white supremacist discourse by encouraging readers to gawk at (as opposed to critically interrogate) the absurdity of right-wing trolling and racist memes, profiling alt-right personalities, and inviting white nationalists to debate under the banner of free speech—all of this under the misguided assumption that their ideas would wither under public scrutiny.[63] Instead, neo-Nazis and white nationalists were giddy with the newfound public attention and used it as a recruitment tool. Thus, Phillips and Milner propose the metaphor of digital *ecologies* and *ecosystems* to illustrate the patterns of influence and interdependence that shape the growth and evolution of far-right ideologies on digital platforms, and how they interact with other media ecosystems and vise-versa. Likewise, an ecological model also accounts for the diffuse and fragmented character of white nationalist digital rhetoric. Rhetorical scholarship on *rhetorical ecologies* highlights how a static conception of rhetorical situations (consisting of stable and discrete elements, such as rhetor, audience, message, and exigence) fail to account for the circulation of distributed rhetorical elements and affect across public networks.[64] As Jenny Edbauer explains, the move from rhetorical situations to rhetorical ecologies "recontextualizes rhetoric in their temporal, historical, and lived fluxes."[65] Drawing from these diverse yet complimentary ecological perspectives of rhetoric and media studies, we argue that manifestos are not discrete and isolated species of texts but rather rhetorically diffuse elements of an interconnected biome, polluted by white nationalist thought. An ecological approach "encourage[s] reflections about how deeply intertwined we are with our world and with one another," and further how digital "pollution" or "toxins"—disinformation and misinformation—affects our collective health and interdependence.[66] For instance, polluted information that filters into one part of a root system might appear in another grove, traveling in sometimes unintended and highly unpredictable ways. From an ecological perspective, it does not matter whether a racist meme or conspiracy theory was circulated as a joke or where it originated—whether it was sincere or satire—pollution always has cascading and highly unpredictable effects on ecosystems that are not easily contained. Moreover, the negative consequences are the same: the people affected by pollution—material or metaphorical—are usually the most vulnerable and marginalized.

Similar to natural ecosystems, digital ecosystems are self-organized, scalable, interdependent, and sustainable.[67] Participation within a given digital ecosystem requires both collaboration and competition within the parameters of informal rules, logics, and acceptable methods of interaction. Conceptualized as ecosystems, far-right digital communities start to resemble a self-organized system designed to assimilate and radicalize curious visitors while repelling stultified outsiders. Additionally, we contend that the language of ecology draws attention to how the atmosphere and environment of a far-right space encourages users to adapt and evolve in order to survive and thrive. In more concrete terms, the manifestos we examine herein are *memetic*, meaning not only that they are composed of specific insider references to racist memes and jokes but also that they represent a unit of cultural transmission, passed from one individual to another by way of imitation.[68] As Derek M. Sparby writes, "Memetic behaviors" are "actions and behaviors recapitulated in new but relevant contexts."[69] That is, memetic communication is a repetition with a difference that summarizes and restates previous utterances but in new circumstances. Memetic discourse involves both imitation and invention so that "over time the meaning itself can evolve and develop a second, coded layer that is undecipherable to normies and newbies, or group outsiders."[70] As Heather Suzanne Woods and Leslie A. Hahner put it, "The rhetorical action of memes is both to normalize and generate devotion to extremism but also to organize and congeal the Alt-right and its modes of publicity."[71] Accompanied by spectacular acts of violence, these manifestos are designed to memetically spread far-right ideas rapidly, entertain insiders, stultify outsiders, and encourage others to join or follow suit.

White terrorist manifestos are dangerous because they facilitate the evolution of white nationalist ideologies that glorify political violence. Although white terrorists draw their vernacular and topics from rhetorical commonplaces, such as the 4chan board /pol/ (politically incorrect), each new shooter draws inspiration and borrows significant portions of text from previous manifestos. For instance, the Christchurch shooter manifesto has become a touchstone for imitators, who not only mimic its style and form but plagiarize entire sections of the manuscript—an internet practice often referred to as "copypasta" (the subject of chapter 4). Much like users adapt images and meme templates to convey new content, each new manifesto is an elaboration and evolution of a previous point of articulation. While an outsider might find this practice mind-numbingly unoriginal and derivative, those familiar with internet culture will immediately recognize the practice as *memetic* (an organizing practice for creating easily spreadable content), *dissociative* (reflective of a radical playpen environment in which everything is a punchline for lulz), and *divisive* (it separates the ingroup from the outgroup). The larger purpose of this memetic practice is to encourage others to imitate their behavior and lower the threshold for violence. Manifestos are not simply reflections of internet culture; they are rhetorical forms that spread toxicity and pollution throughout digital ecosystems with real-world, violent consequences.

PUBLIC MURDER AND GENRES OF POLITICAL VIOLENCE

Our attention to white terrorist manifestos is motivated by a concern with *form* as the rhetorical adhesive that makes white supremacist ideology stick.[72] By form, we are referring to recognizable patterns of discourse—speech and expressive conduct—that recur within the public imaginary in response to common types of rhetorical situations. Often labeled "genres," forms are not simply objective classifications for types of discourse but instead patterned forms of social action that address common rhetorical exigencies.[73] Genres are conceptual structures that can be populated with specific symbolic content and are organized in such a way as to be recognizable and responsive to audiences' needs and desires. At the same time, forms predicate the kind of content that comes to populate them, meaning that they contain particular affordances that dictate how discourses can function and circulate.[74] A meme, for example, has a lower barrier to participation, can be reproduced and spread quickly, and tends to reduce social complexities to truncated, polarizing, and sometimes glib interpretations. Structurally speaking, memes are a poor format for deep, philosophical inquiry. They are, unfortunately, an ideal format for racism, vitriol, and enmity. Joshua Gunn conceives of genres as a kind of "affective apparatus," meaning that different forms cultivate and translate the ineffable, felt intensities of the body into language.[75] In courting audience expectations and desire, forms condition not only symbolic but even visceral registers to a particular discursive and representational pattern. For instance, certain film genres (horror, melodrama, pornography) are even maligned for addressing the body of the spectator and inducing an involuntary memetic response.[76]

Manifesting Violence posits that an emphasis on form is a particularly fruitful way of understanding how the rhetoric of the far-right enables political violence. For instance, the ad nauseum repetition of white supremacist memes does not so much build a rational argument for violence as much as the practice invites derealization, or psychic dissociation, from the real-world consequences of symbolic and physical violence. Likewise, manifestos that are composed of racist memetic discourse translate inchoate feelings of personal rage into the political language of pogroms and sadistic violence. The white terrorist manifesto has augmented the form by mixing personal grievances and prejudices with an ensemble of internet jokes, memetic references, and other transgressive modes of address. In foregrounding a relationship between racist violence and entertainment, these manifestos court audience enjoyment of white supremacy. As we explain below, enjoyment names not only the register of entertainment, but instead the psychoanalytic concept of *jouissance*, or the ecstatic pleasure-in-pain garnered from the compulsive repetition of traumatic and unpleasant experiences. Regardless of deliberate racist commitments, white supremacist manifestos attempt to stoke audience desires to imitate and repeat as part of how prospective recruits comes to constitute themselves as members of the in-group, the white nation.

Herein, we attend to form in two senses. First, we argue that the genre of the digital manifesto amplifies the affective intensity of replacement rhetoric and fantasies of racial retribution. A manifesto is a familiar and powerful rhetorical form, or genre, in which those who typically experience exclusion lay bare the contradictions of democratic culture through a bitter jeremiad or radical invective. As Janet Lyon observes, manifestos participate "in a reduced understanding of heterogeneous social fields, creating audiences through a rhetoric of exclusivity, parceling out political identities across a polarized discursive field, claiming for 'us' the moral high ground of revolutionary idealism, and constructing 'them' as ideological tyrants, bankrupt usurpers, or corrupt fools."[77] Manifestos are also disruptive rhetorical acts that mark a felt urgency for revolution over reform.[78] As José Ángel Maldonado puts it, "manifestos are rhetorical texts designed to rupture the 'now.'"[79] They do so by amplifying social antagonisms between "the people" and "the elite," and, in turn, disrupt conventional political logic and articulate a radical demand. Although there are exceptions, manifestos have typically been associated with leftist populism or progressive political movements composed by individuals from historically marginalized groups.

Recognizing the rhetorical power of the genre, white terrorists have appropriated manifestos to articulate their political subjectivity, justify violence, and encourage imitation. With traits of hierarchy, exclusivity, and polarity, manifestos affirm an identity grounded in political exile and enacted through violence. It is no coincidence that white nationalists have seized the genre to channel white fantasies of racial retribution. White terrorist manifestos condense, distill, and oversimplify social antagonisms, which enable them to conflate their authors' felt sense of marginalization and alienation with systemic "material victimhood."[80] In other words, they employ the form to politicize their personal failings and prejudices, constitute an aggrieved white political identity, and enact this identity through public murder. As Richard Branscomb writes, "Part of the seductive appeal of the manifesto genre is that it facilitates political extremists to manifest the 'truth' of their selves as individual embodiments of their hateful political movement."[81] White terrorists frame virtually all personal struggles—from their failures in school, work, or dating—as a synecdoche for an organized and structural dispossession of white people. The manifesto warrants this conflation by constructing the enemy in racist tropes drawn from the symbolic economy of chattel slavery, nativism, and colonialism; however, in his analysis of the El Paso manifesto, Richard Pineda argues that the text also reflects the immediate discursive fields sowed by President Trump and the far-right's racist caricatures of Latinx "invaders" and calls for political violence.[82]

Pineda's most insightful argument, that we draw from here, is that the assailant's performance of physical violence should be analyzed as an extension of the speech act advanced in the manifesto.[83] Consequently, manifestos do not simply warrant racist violence, they are part of *one speech act* that we refer to throughout this book as *public murder*.[84] Public murder, we contend, is an extremist rhetorical enactment of political sovereignty that renders its targets into fungible chattel so as to nourish the life and community of a privileged citizenry. As Jay Childers observes, such violence is often described as "senseless"; however, he explains that "physical violence has a purpose, and that purpose is . . . rhetorical."[85] Or to appropriate Marshall McLuhan, the violence *is* the message. Public murder is a genre of expressive conduct that merges hate speech (racist memes, online screeds, manifestos) with physical violence for the purpose of establishing a community's sovereign authority—in this case, the white nation. The physical act of killing is the tactile application of symbolic violence to other bodies that produces "alien" subjects and conveys their fungibility, their absence of humanity. As Lisa Corrigan writes, "The gun itself functions as an extension and protection of whiteness," meaning that to fire a gun into a crowd of "invaders" is to manifest racist conceptions of property and propriety over public space in a material way.[86] White terrorist manifestos are part of a killing assemblage: the aggregation of violent tropes and fantasies subsequently put into practice by the physical act of maiming and murder. As Lydia Wilkes, Nate Kreuter, and Ryan Skinnel put it, "The [white supremacist] message is carried not through the vibrations of speech nor the scratches of writing, but out of the barrel of [a] gun."[87] The texts we analyze do not begin and end in a word-processing document—they are honed in advance within far-right digital ecologies and made manifest through bullets, shrapnel, and gore. Following Bryan McCann's reading of serial killer Ted Bundy's murders as a kind rhetorical enactment of modernity's drive to violently control femininity, we find symbolic resonance and continuity between the writings and representations of mass murders and their physical enactments.[88] Public murder is also memetic insofar as it functions as a unit of cultural transmission: a genre of speech plus conduct that can be imitated, repeated, elaborated, and spread virally.

As E. Chebrolu observes, white terrorist manifestos are composed of racist signifiers incessantly intoned in the digital ecologies of 4chan and 8chan to interpellate white nationalist subjects. These far-right digital ecologies build a white political identity grounded in anti-Blackness.[89] A phobic reaction to people of color treading into spaces of white sovereignty, manifestos give stability to whiteness as both a political identity and a signifier of humanness.[90] Such documents offer to reveal a series of racial "truths," drawn from an unconscious repository of racist "knowledge," that help belabor associations between whiteness and naturalness, inevitability, and superiority. As Chebrolu observes, liberal critics of white terrorist manifestos tend to decouple whiteness from white nationalism, instead portraying the killers as being motivated by individual pathologies.[91] What these critics miss is that in seeking out racial "knowledge," manifestos actually build political white kinship networks that, through vigilant acts of self-sacrifice, maintain the symbolic affinity structures that underwrite an anti-Black world. Manifestos assemble and archive textual fragments of white nationalist rhetoric and serve as repositories of racist tropes that ground murder as a form of social action in service of the white nation. Such *political* violence is expressive conduct, a physical extension of the racist fantasies and white kinship structures conveyed in the manifestos. Therefore, these texts unify disparate strands of white nationalist discourse from across the internet and condense them into a unified assemblage of violence. That is, public murder memes bring white nationalist political identity into existence.

Our second concept of form concerns how racist tropes cement white supremacist ideology through repetition. From the Greek word *topos*, tropes indicate a "turning toward," or in the direction of something, a recurring pattern of symbolic activity (speech, writing, images) that connects signifiers with referents. According to Christian Lundberg, there are both general economies of tropes (metaphor, metonymy, synecdoche, catachresis, irony) and specific economies of tropes (associations within a particular contextual field, such as "might makes right," or "childhood is innocence").[92] Drawing from Lacanian psychoanalysis, Lundberg argues that because language cannot offer unicity or coherence, subjects necessarily labor and invest in the arbitrary and accidental pathways forged between signifiers. Tropes are indications that no connection between signifiers is guaranteed in advance and that only through compulsive repetition are those connections made durable. Lundberg notes, "A theory of trope ought to gain primacy in rhetorical theory, because trope is always immanent within and constitutes the specific contexts where persuasion, identification, propriety, or any of the other readily available rhetorical means for understanding the function of discourse are operative."[93] Like other forms, tropes also garner profound affective investments—or a felt intensity toward the stability of signifying chains—because they provide an illusory constancy in our symbolic and imaginary realities.

The tropology of modern racism is underwritten by a series of arbitrary yet sedimented associations between whiteness and humanness, on the one hand, and dark skin and abjection, animality, primitivism, criminality, and inferiority, on the other.[94] Stuart Hall, for instance, calls race a "sliding signifier" that references not biological facts but instead "systems of meaning that have come to be fixed in classification of culture."[95] Race itself is a trope for classifying bodies according to arbitrary markers of difference (skin color, phenotype) on a sliding scale from human to nonhuman.[96] Within this tropological economy of difference, whiteness has been overrepresented as the exemplary form of human, while Blackness has been perpetually relegated to "flesh."[97] Highlighting the general economy of tropes, such as metonymy and catachresis, Calvin Warren and Saidiya Hartman have illustrated how the symbolic economy of chattel slavery misappropriated Blackness as a *vehicle* for white capital, property, and sentiments.[98] Eugenics, phrenology, and other forms of racist population science also rely on specific economy tropes, such as *mongrelization,* to denote a sedimented connection between interracial sexuality and the degradation of white racial stock. It is for this reason that Watts argues that modern racist tropology is not so much a marker of difference as much as it is a marker of *degeneration* and decay, whereby difference is a signifier of abjection.[99] Allison L. Rowland observes how tropes concerning race, ability, sexuality, and gender set the terms for inclusion into the category of human, or what lives count as valuable lives and which lesser forms of life are to be treated as threats to more valuable forms of life.[100] Building on this observation, we contend that replacement rhetoric functions as a racist "biotrope," or "zoetrope," meaning that it is a repertoire of discursive resources that can be summoned to associate racial difference with degradation, contamination, and death. Biotropes mobilize affective economies of anti-Blackness to produce dangerous bodies "against which the nation-state must gird itself."[101] The rhetoric of replacement mobilizes stock racist biotropes that render bodies into signifiers of hypersexuality, criminality, disease, and malevolence. The manifestos we examine sediment these arbitrary bodily signifiers into a code, or a system of meaning, that helps manage the threat of difference and securitize the white nation.

Ultimately, replacement rhetoric garners affective intensity because its proponents capitalize upon the *repetition* of form: the incessant reiteration of connections between signifiers and patterns of discourse that evince the necessity of habituated pathways of meaning to organize our symbolic life. Where genres such as a manifestos channel white personal grievances into a violent political language, racial biotropes connect racialized bodies with signifiers of death, decay, and abjection. The compulsive repetition of both forms organize white enjoyment of racist violence—not solely in the sense of entertainment but instead the Lacanian notion of *jouissance*, or a kind of ecstatic pleasure-in-pain, experienced in the compulsive repetition of unpleasant or transgressive experiences.[102] The far right's tropology stages an encounter with the markers of abjection (death, decay, contamination) that threaten the subject's undoing and serves as a reminder of the void of meaning and identity that precedes the subject's entry into the symbolic.[103] *Jouissance* does not denote joy or pleasure (*plaisur*), but instead an obscene yet elusive gratification beyond Freud's pleasure principle that is reaped through transgressions of conventions.[104] Lacan's *objet petit a,* otherwise known as the "lost object," refers to a fantasy of unmediated gratification (*jouissance*) and wholeness that preceded the paternal demand that subjects enter the symbolic and become social subjects.[105] Cut off from *jouissance*, subjects are compelled to compulsively repeat painful or ecstatic experiences that transgress the law and conventions installed by the introduction of the signifier. Indeed, we can find in internet culture various forms of obscene *jouissance* in everything from the petty transgressions of racist humor to violent diatribes that unabashedly endorse genocidal violence. As Terry Eagleton puts it, ultimate *jouissance* is that "which persuades us to reap a perverse gratification from our own destruction. The sniggering and buffoonery of the damned signify the mockery of those who know that everything is entirely futile."[106] Far-right internet culture's play in the shocking and forbidden racist signifiers, and their compulsive repetition through memetic discourse, constitute an audience hailed and bound together through the shared experience of racist *jouissance*.

Racist *jouissance* is an affect garnered by staging encounters with the abject threat of race and flirting with the possibility of real-world violence. As Derek Hook argues, "Racist *jouissance* . . . is never simply a spontaneous individual psychological reaction. It is, by contrast, conditioned by precise historical and symbolic conditions . . . the threat that the racial order is thought to pose is invariably defined relative to the ego-ideals of a given society, to those symbolic values for which members of the society are willing to live and die for."[107] Thus, manifestos and racist tropes create the conditions for white audiences to *enjoy* racist violence insofar as enjoyment connotes a compulsive drive to repetitively transgresses the law, social conventions, and cultural prohibitions in pursuit of an illusory sense of unicity.[108] In doing so, the forms adopted by white supremacists invite repetition and imitation to garner affective investments in violence as a necessary and legitimate form of securitization.

CHAPTER PREVIEWS

In the chapters that follow, we critically analyze the manifestos of white terrorists and the white nationalist digital ecologies in which they were radicalized. Each chapter explores how different aspects of white supremacist digital culture contribute to the overall function of these texts. We explore the contours of the rapidly mutating and evolving nature of white supremacy, particularly when digital communication enters the material world as racist violence. White terrorist manifestos reflect and reinforce the intensification of online white supremacy, and, like all memes, these texts are units of cultural transmission that survive by imitation, adaptation, and elaboration. In our analysis, we have made several choices about how to represent appeals to mass violence ethically. First, we have chosen not to use the names of the shooters themselves but instead only to refer to them by the names of locations. Our rationale is that we do not want to contribute to the assailants' efforts at martyrdom and fame. Second, we are cautious about the replication of memetic content. Despite the widespread availability of these documents, we have chosen not to visually represent racist memes so as not to contribute directly to their shareability.

For analytical purposes, we do attend to how particular memetic references work in a generalizable sense and attempt to explain why those references are commonly repeated across manifestos.

Decoding memetic references is essential to unraveling the ciphers and booby traps laid by white terrorists to foil and subvert outgroups who encounter these texts. We contend that acts of criticism and interpretation help defamiliarize racist tropes and explain why they resonate with potential audiences. We are guided by Kenneth Burke's efforts to demystify the contemptible prose of Hitler's *Mein Kampf*, offering resources to contest racism, violence, and white nationalism. In Burke's essay, he argued that we must understand "what kind of 'medicine' this medicine-man has concocted" if we are to "forestall the concocting of similar medicine in America."[109] Indeed, it is true that these are dangerous texts. It is also equally true that the genie cannot be put back into the bottle, no matter how often Google or social media platforms scrub their sites and search engines. We are compelled to critique these texts as a scholarly intervention into the escalation of white radicalization and violence. To ignore these texts is to do so at our own peril.

Chapter 1 begins with an examination of the replacement theory as a revival and repackaging of biotropes of antimiscegenation, amalgamation, and hypersexuality derived from the history of chattel slavery and nativism in the US. These tropes transform immigrant bodies and the bodies of people of color into bioweapons: bodies whose excess of fertility threatens to overwhelm and dilute the purity of white racial stock. We examine how two specific tropes—the high fertility immigrant and the innocent white child—dehumanize people of color, while investing whiteness with metaphysical, ontological, and biological essence. Chapter 2 attends to how these killers glorify violence and suicide as pathways to empowerment in an age of declining white upward mobility. This chapter takes up two tropes of defensive violence: antiheroism and necroempowerment. White terrorists portray themselves as charismatic outlaws who destabilize the bankrupt morality of late capitalism, exploiting contemporary televisual culture's fascination with violent yet sympathetic antiheroes. These killers glorify targeted racist violence and self-sacrifice as an expression of self-mastery, self-love, and martyrdom. Drawing from Sayak Valencia's theorization of *gore capitalism*, we argue that white terrorist manifestos illustrate how the digital far right's glorification of death and gore derealize violence and provide whiteness with metaphysical grandeur.

Chapter 3 analyzes the manifestos of three eco-fascist mass shooters, the killers at Christchurch, El Paso, and Buffalo, in order to decode the tropology of ecofascism, a far-right ideology that intertwines racial pseudoscience with environmentalism. These men committed unprompted, deadly attacks on people of color for the stated purpose of accelerating racial conflicts. Moreover, they each authored manifestos meant to describe their commitment to ecofascist ideology, justify killing and harming innocent people, and inspire more racist violence against people of color. We argue that these three ecofascist manifestos function as digital jeremiads, or rhetorical arguments that justify public murder, by contextualizing them within a strategy of anticapitalist ecological accelerationism, wherein all violence has the potential to be revolutionary. By understanding these manifestos as a type of jeremiad, we forward an understanding of the genre within the context of online cultures and consider the ways in which eco-ascist appeals to violence are symptomatic of the differentiated ecologies of the internet.

Chapter 4 examines the traces of far-right digital ecologies that radicalize young white men, particularly reflected in the use of memes, inside jokes, and "copypasta" (blocks of text copied and pasted across the internet used to annoy outsiders and entertain insider audiences). The purpose of these digital practices is to encourage imitation, improvisation, and elaboration—practices that establish a user's ethos within particular digital ecologies. Manifestos are riddled with insider references that transform violence into something that seems entertaining, countercultural, and even humorous. Repeated ad nauseum, memetic references and practices are thought to indoctrinate and radicalize audiences, inviting new users to participate in the spread of white supremacist propaganda. We argue that to their audiences these memetic references and inside jokes contained in these manifestos make white supremacy seem hip and fun while dissociating users from real-world consequences of violence.

Finally, in the epilogue we focus on the political and electoral implications of replacement rhetoric, with a particular focus on the legacy of white supremacist violence in the West and the possibilities of future violence. We attend to the accelerating drumbeat of mass violence that now organizes public life and the role that far-right digital ecologies play in the rhetorical production of terror. We discuss the implications of the mainstreaming of replacement theory and suggest that the demographic panic will continue to bolster an increasingly paranoid iteration of whiteness. We conclude by discussing the concrete challenges of deradicalization and resisting digital hate speech, particularly where few good policy alternatives exist. Ultimately, our goal in analyzing these manifestos is to help decipher far-right digital ecologies and equip readers with the critical insights to confront violent white supremacy in the twenty-first century.

1

Erotic Racism and White Futurity

THE US CENSUS Bureau has projected that by 2042, the US will be a "majority-minority" nation, with whites accounting for less than 50 percent of the national population.[1] Social psychologists Maureen A. Craig and Jennifer A. Richeson found that when whites were exposed to these projections, they were more likely to express negative attitudes toward Latinx, Black, and Asian Americans in addition to expressing preference for interactions within their own ethnic group.[2] On a larger scale, evidence of the impending demographic shift has intensified the pressure on white political elites to consolidate power further through tax reductions on inherited wealth, industry deregulation, redlining, charter schools, gerrymandering, and voter disenfranchisement.[3] Indeed, Trump and the far right harnessed the rhetoric of victimhood to invite white publics to think of themselves as structurally oppressed by the relative gains of racial minorities and, therefore, entitled to an even larger share of public attention, moral authority, and economic resources.[4] Thus, as Linda Alcoff observes, the threat that power may soon be redistributed along new racial and geographic lines—as remote as that threat might be—has engendered a white reaction that can be characterized as "hysterical."[5]

The rhetoric of replacement offers a framework for white publics to interpret demographic shifts as a well-orchestrated plan to eradicate white people and replace them with high-fertility immigrants. Such racist paranoia represents a much longer historical trajectory of nativism and xenophobia that is underwritten by constructions of pathologically violent and sexually excessive bodies—a series of blackening *biotropes* deployed to contain racial others who threaten white economic, social, and political dominance.[6] Such phobias become particularly acute when demographic shifts threaten to reshape the distribution of power, requiring cycles of securitization and militarization to protect white sovereignty. As Ronald W. Greene's rhetorical history of turn-of-the-century population science in the US illustrates, xenophobia and low white fertility rates, alongside the rise of the eugenics movement and the institutionalization of demography, amplified the racial logics of biopolitical governmentality, wherein threats of white "racial suicide" and the contamination of national bloodlines legitimized increasingly extreme state-based interventions.[7] Over a century later, a similar demographic panic helps account for the surge in white nationalist movements, white terrorism and vigilantism, and the further militarization of law enforcement and immigration policy. What is ultimately at stake is not merely political and economic power but the *symbolic* power of white identity and white futurity in a multiracial America.

To begin our interrogation of white terrorist manifestos, we attend to the racist tropology of the "high fertility" or hypersexual immigrant who animates these alleged or convicted killers. To this end, white terrorist manifestos express a pathological fixation with Black, Latinx, and Muslim sexuality and sexual reproduction, evidenced in lengthy diatribes about the threat of hypersexuality, hyperfertility, interracial sex, pedophilia, rape, and incest. In this chapter, we contend that the rhetoric of white genocide is as much an imagined sexual panic as it is a real one. That is, replacement rhetoric *eroticizes* racism through obscene accounts of bodies overflowing with sexual and reproductive excess. To name this fixation as erotic racism is to illustrate a well-worn though facile connection between Blackness, race, and white desire, or, more specifically, an ambivalence within the white imaginary in relation to its own prurient and sinister fantasies.[8] We specifically attend to two figural markers of ambivalent desire that reappear throughout white terrorist manifestos: the high-fertility immigrant and the white child. The high-fertility immigrant represents sexual excess in terms of a surplus capacity to reproduce populations whose mere existence is a threat to white life. By contrast, the white child is an antipodal figure whose presumed innocence and asexuality consummate fantasies of white futurity and whose defense sanctifies white violence.

In this chapter, we argue that the demand to secure "a future for white children" is not simply a call to arms that validates racist violence, but is also a trope that aligns white violence with a broader biopolitical vision of an ethnostate charged with the sovereign authority to manage the racial and sexual health of the population in the name of white life.[9] This white supremacist slogan conjures these antipodal figures as objects of taboo knowledge that renew and resecuritize white sovereignty against demographic and sexual threats. Although Michel Foucault's conception of biopolitics is most conspicuously marked by the injunction to "make live and let die," Mbembe reminds us that sovereignty also consists of "the capacity to kill so as to live."[10] A charge to assert demographic supremacy, "securing a future for white children," functions tropologically to consolidate racial and sexual investment into a fantasy of white futurity. Understanding racial replacement rhetoric as both a race and sex panic evinces what Ian Barnard characterizes as a "morphing typology" to name how sex panics index other allusive and unnamed anxieties, including queerphobia and racism.[11] In this case, the morphology works in the other direction, where a racial panic also concerns unnamed sexual anxieties about the proper object of white nationalist desire. White terrorist manifestos beseech white subjects to coordinate their racial affinities with their sexual affinities to reproduce white life. The white child's sanctification in this project ratifies the centrality of proper heteronormative desire to white futurity while its sexual endangerment legitimizes racist subjugation and extermination of racial Others in the name of sanctified white life.

In this regard, white terrorist manifestos also resound and amplify the right's general preoccupation with perceived sexual impropriety, marked elsewhere by the proliferation of bills criminalizing transgender and gender-affirming health care, drag shows, and reproductive freedom, alongside growing adherence to conspiracy theories positing that the US government is run by a secret cabal of Satan-worshiping pedophiles. We contend that the resonance between replacement conspiracies and moral panics about deviant sexualities illustrate how the figure of the white child—threatened by all manner of sexual perversion—authorizes forms of sovereignty premised on killing to make live. The white child also cements the connection between white supremacy and heteronormativity; a connection made explicit within far-right digital ecosystem issuing the "white baby challenge" and generating attendant discourse encouraging healthy white couples to procreate excessivley in response to the impending demographic shift.[12] Reflecting the assailants' radicalization on /pol/, we contend that these manifestos showcase the far right's efforts to consolidate tropes of biological racism with sexual deviance to reinvigorate whiteness as a site of racial, national, and sexual identification. At the same time, expressing investments in the innocent and presexual white child help subjects disavow the dimensions of sexual desire elicited by a fixation with the sexual predilection of racial Others.

RACIAL AND SEXUAL EXCESS

In his groundbreaking *Black Skins, White Masks,* Frantz Fanon satirizes white fears of Black sexuality: "As for the Negroes, they are sexually promiscuous. Not surprisingly, running around like that in the bush! Apparently they fornicate just about everywhere and at all times. They're sexual beasts. They have so many children they've lost count. If we're not careful they'll inundate us with little mulattoes."[13] While Fanon's intentions were clearly ironic, the Christchurch shooter embraces these fears literally: "I believe racial differences exist between peoples and they have a great impact on the way we shape our societies. I also believe fertility rates are part of those racial differences and that the immigrants in our lands with high fertility must be forced out to ensure the existance [*sic*] of our race. So yes. I am a racist."[14]

The manifesto of the Christchurch assailant—the shooter who killed fifty-one and injured forty-nine people at the Al Noor Mosque in Christchurch, New Zealand—shares much in common with Fanon's caricature of white phobic preoccupations with the supposed excessive fertility of Black and Brown people. From different vantage points, both passages cite the historical construction of Black and Brown people as hypersexual, primitive, and overflowing with fertility. Their seemingly innate capacity for sexual reproduction prefigures their bodies as weapons—their very survival is posited as a long-term threat to white civilization. As Judith Butler has contended, such arguments fit within racial schemas of self-defense wherein white lives register more "emphatically as lives" than immigrants and persons of color.[15] Hence, we juxtapose these two passages to highlight how the historical-racial schema advanced by the replacement myth is trapped in an ambivalent relationship with a white nationalist's imaginary's construction of the sexuality of racial others.[16] That is to say that the flip side of fear and disgust is the desire *to be the Other* and to *possess the Other* inasmuch as the Other's sexuality consummates a fantasy of a complete satisfaction, alongside a vision of heteronormative reproductive white futurity underwritten by the innocent white child. Echoing Fanon, Tommy J. Curry explains that the erotic and homoerotic are "an inextricable aspect of racial psychology, power, and White men's desire to determine the Black male body's uses."[17] As such, the rhetoric of replacement names the inexorable and uncanny relationship between racial fear and sexual desire. This relationship underscores that the rhetoric of replacement must construct fantasies of hypersexual racial Others but also fantasies about the proper object of white masculine desire: white women. Investment in the latter helps disavow the uneasy fear of the former—containment and control of interracial sexuality desublimates the eroticism of the entire enterprise into the reproduction of white children. The racial tropes that underlie demographic paranoia are inherited from the symbolic economy of white supremacy, slavery, eugenics, and imperialism, or what Stuart Hall refers to as a series of sliding signifiers that manifest as "the biological trace that remains in racialized discourse of today."[18] Onto this Other—the buck, the dark-skinned rapist, the high fertility immigrant—white nationalists have projected a sexual dynamic that reverses historical power relations of colonialism that depended on the systematic rape and forced marriage of indigenous people and women of color.[19] These inverted fantasies of interracial sexual violation conceal and disavow the original sexual trauma of the nation's founding.

But the only way this Other's enjoyment is accessible to the white nationalist imagination is through a rhetoric of projection, or failed attribution, wherein white subjects imagine racial Others as enjoying some desired object but in a way in which they themselves have been prohibited from enjoying desired objects. According to Jean Laplanche and Jean-Bertrand Pontalis, projection is an "operation whereby qualities, feelings, wishes, or even 'objects,' which the subject refuses to recognize or rejects in himself, are expelled from the self and located in another person or thing." [20] The so-called high-fertility immigrant figures as such a projection, yet its flesh-and-blood materialization is more likely to be targeted for sexual, racial, and administrative violence than ordinary white citizens, evidenced by the persistent sexual abuse and brutality administered by militarized law enforcement agencies.[21] But as Todd McGowan argues about projection, xenophobes and nativists who enjoy enormous privileges relative to more precarious populations nonetheless envision "the illegal immigrant awash in a linguistic and cultural enjoyment that excludes natives."[22] Likewise, Fanon contends that white people often operate as if Black and Brown subjects have particular desires and sexual capacities, yet they are in fact mirrors of the white subject's own desire. Moreover, Chebrolu reminds us that in the context of white nationalism, the "enjoying other" can be read as a fantasy assembled from networks of signifiers and "circuits of desire" culled from the historic violence of chattel slavery and imperialism that treat flesh as if it were innately meaningful.[23]

These networks of desire also overlap with other native tropes and projection devices concerning the pollution of national bloodlines, racial hybridity, rape, and the excessive fertility of immigrants. The racial anxiety exhibited by white nationalists reflects the failure of these (post)racial signifiers to guarantee a stable white identity in a globalized, multicultural future. Hence, these manifestos all reference the waning significance of white racial identification as a crisis of paternal authority and construct racial others as barriers to white enjoyment. But it is the recognition that whiteness is simply *an* object, rather than a transcendent universal or stable anchor of identity, that thwarts the white subject's drive for coherence. It is this anxiety that causes fantasies to break down and the enclosure of the enjoying other produces the conditions of violence—or the prefiguring of the racialized body as subject to pure violence.[24]

Attending to the figure of the high-fertility immigrant illustrates the unique conceptions of racial-sexual desire that underwrites the present demographic panic. Even as racial Others provoke fear and revulsion, they are imagined to have an ability to partake in sexual and reproductive behaviors that so-called "civilized" subjects are barred from indulging in. More importantly, racism is a projection and displacement of those desires onto racialized

Others. To quote Curry once more, racial otherness becomes "fungible, bending to the desire-fear of the White society that surrounds him."[25] These insights illustrate how the borders of white sovereignty are redrawn through phobic reactions to the biological excesses of Black and Brown people. The erotic entailments of racism demand both a disavowal and return of the phobic object—a process by which anxiety is domesticated but never fully allayed. The white genocide myth articulates fantasies of an enjoying Other who appears to (but of course does not) have unfettered access to *jouissance*. McGowan argues that such fantasies are the source material for racial violence that are repetitively "directed toward the other who appears as a barrier to the subject's enjoyment."[26] In other words, the outcome of this rhetoric is quite frequently a form of violence that compensates, though temporarily, for the "exigence of the death drive."[27] So put, if the Other were not so proximate and their presence not so overwhelming, whites would have a future.

The white nationalist imaginary is ironically dependent on a racialized and sexualized conception of incommensurate difference. This objectification of racial otherness engenders a sense of mastery and control over the phobic object. Thus, the fantasy of being inundated by "little mulattoes" articulates excessive fertility as a biological threat—one in which interracial sex threatens to annihilate white civilization. Here, we analyze the present cycle of racial-sexual anxieties because the white nationalist speaks directly to the question of white desire for self-mastery. The attribution of hypersexuality to Black and Brown people is, above all, a projection of desire onto the Other whose demands are unintelligible and beyond control. White desire for the Other, he observes, corresponds with white men's pathological fixation with a primal past wherein subjects purportedly experienced an uninterrupted satisfaction of the drives—a past that seems to constitute racialized subject's ontological condition in the present. In short, the fantasy of repulsion is a token of desire for the Other's enjoyment. The rhetoric of replacement both attributes desire *to* the other and channels desire *for* the Other in the form of a violent demand. Thought of in this manner, replacement rhetoric evinces how the present demographic panic sutures white futurity to racial and sexual delusions that entail inevitable violence.[28]

The high-fertility immigrant is antipodal to the figure of the white child, a kind of cipher onto which others are free to project prohibited desires so that they may be repressed and disavowed. In this way, the white child helps resolve this ambivalent fixation with the high-fertility immigrant through a sanctified fantasy of white futurity. In the manifestos examined herein, sex, reproduction, and violence are twined in a project to preserve an image of completeness in the yet-to-be white child. At the same time, white children are also in peril: they are supposedly victimized by foreign sexual predators, threatened by senseless acts of terrorism, and denied a future by the failure to be produced. The trope of the innocent yet vulnerable child is pliable to an endless number of political endeavors that expand the scope of state power to police, regulate, and discipline deviance. As Bryan J. McCann observes, "the trope of the Child is ubiquitous and powerful in its capacity to constitute and mobilize publics."[29] A fixation of heterosexual culture, the child metonymizes sacred moral virtues, such as innocence, purity, and asexuality. However, as Lauren Berlant observes, childhood is an adult fantasy the consummation of which mandates the cleansing of public culture of adult desires in order to protect heteronormative institutions.[30] White childhood is particularly sanctified; it is the site of overlapping racial and sexual investments in the fantasy of innocence.[31] Indeed, one need look no further than the culture of lynching and the myth of the Black rapist to grasp the common ideological lineage shared by discourses of racial and sexual "purity."[32] In the rhetoric of replacement, the *a*sexuality of the endangered white child stands in stark contrast to the excessive sexuality of racial others. In the name of the white child, violence is presumed to be sanctified. But we also want to suggest that the white child signifies a number of other important affective investments in whiteness. Namely, the white child is also an image of completeness in its closeness to unmediated enjoyment. Evacuated of and protected from adult desires, the white child's asexuality represents a kind of pure potential that operates in these manifestos to restabilize white as a signifier. In other words, investments in the endangered child also operate to purify whiteness of its sexual perversions, while childlessness represents both hedonism and a sexual divestment from white identity.

As a source of affective investment, these manifestos summon the threat of the pedophile and lionize the child as a figure who redeems a broken and innocent conception of whiteness. As Erin Rand argues, "It is precisely the impression of purity, wholesomeness, and virginal artlessness that make children so titillating to adult fantasy, so the 'sacred' child figure both entangles children in circuits of adult desire while also denying childhood's own queerness."[33] If we take white terrorists' invocations of the innocent-yet-endangered child to signify a coherent and innocent white identity imperiled by the perverse desires of race traitors and the excessive sexuality of racial others, the threat of pedophilia brings an encounter with the image of the child as completeness into vulnerability. This vulnerability, in turn, disavows the queer withdrawal from reproductive futurism that white supremacists find unacceptable about the present condition of whiteness—or white people's refusal to "outproduce" high-fertility cultures. The stakes of protecting the sacred child from perverts is as much about ensuring white futurity as it is about channeling libidinal desires into white supremacy; whiteness itself is already subjected to sexual humiliation. Whiteness must not only be protected from queer and perverse desires but attuned to the useful sublimation of the drives into reproduction.

THE HIGH FERTILITY IMMIGRANT

The Christchurch shooter's manifesto begins with a selection from Welsh poet Dylan Thomas's "Don't Go Gentle into That Good Night," a work Thomas allegedly wrote for his dying father. Each stanza addresses a different masculine persona: "wise men," "good men," "wild men," and finally "grave men."[34] It is this last persona that preoccupies the author: according to him, this persona is a nihilistic, fatalistic, and morally decrepit man of Euro-American culture who, in the author's estimation, is soon to be replaced by the youthful vitality of non-European races. The manifesto commands that these "grave men" to "rage against the dying of the light." The poem announces the manuscript's compulsive rumination on white death and the potent sexuality of dark-skinned bodies that overflow with an excess of fertility. To emphasize the point, the manuscript begins with an incantation: "It's the birthrates. It's the birthrates. It's the birthrates." After a cursory analysis of differential birthrates between whites and immigrant populations, the assailant concluded: "THIS IS WHITE GENOCIDE."[35] Here the author emphatically broadcasts that sexual reproduction—primitive versus the overcivilized libido—is the central racial antagonism between white people and people of color. Immigrants' prolific and fertile bodies are weapons in a war without "a single shot" fired.[36]

As this opening salvo suggests, many white terrorist manifestos are fixated on racial birthrate disparities; a threat that appears in the form of the "high-fertility immigrant." Often referred to as "invaders," high-fertility immigrants constitute a biotrope that sutures together a discourse of scientific racism, nativism, and (white) reproductive futurism, condensing each discursive strand into one figure whose innate reproductive capacities imperil the propagation of white life. The high-fertility immigrant is a conflation of race and culture, a biological essence from which cultural formations emerge to sustain its continued self-propagation, including family values, traditionalism, and collectivism. Although such cultural attributes might be portrayed as virtues when found in white subjects, in the rhetoric of replacement they represent a kind of perverse vitality or life-drive that, in and of itself, constitutes a mortal threat to white existence. The high-fertility immigrant's innate capacity and will to reproduce evokes what Lacan called *hainamoration*, or feelings of simultaneous hatred toward another but love for the object they enjoy.[37] Thus, high-fertility immigrants—animalistic, immoral, promiscuous, and of limited intelligence—must be hated (and killed) because they possess a beloved object.

The high-fertility immigrant represents the "warfare of the cradle," a kind of genocidal violence that is waged through the simple reproduction of life. For instance, the El Paso assailant declares that "invaders . . . have close to the highest birthrate of all ethnicities in America." As a result, "racial diversity will disappear as either race mixing or genocide will take place."[38] Borrowing large portions of the Christchurch manifesto (a common formal practice that will be described in detail in chapter 4), the Buffalo assailant also asserts that "this crisis of mass immigration and sub-replacement fertility is an assault on the European people that, if not combated, will ultimately result in the complete racial and cultural replacement of the European people."[39] The Bratislava assailant concurs with these assessments, but adds an anti-Semitic conspiracy theory, writing that "It's the Jews, It's the Jews, It's the Jews."[40] In all these statements, the assailants cite birthrate disparities as evidence of an ongoing war of attrition, orchestrated by Jewish elites, that harnesses the power of excessive sexuality to breed white civilization out of existence. The assailants liken immigrant sexuality to a kind of fleshy weapon of mass destruction.

Perhaps what is surprising, though reflective of racial discourse /pol/, is that many of the assailants cast white life as weak and lacking in a strong symbolic attachment to racial identity. In other words, one might expect white terrorist manifestos to express comradery and affirm white identity in ways common to places like Stormfront; yet, Chebrolu illustrates how discourse between white nationalists on /pol/ tends to be rivalrous and highlights the improper functioning and failed protection of whiteness.[41] Hence, manifestos tend to lambast other people for not demonstrating a proper and embodied commitment to white futurity. Thus, in our analysis of /pol/, we argue that racial replacement rhetoric is a corrective rhetoric, designed not for the direct purpose of affirming white superiority, but rather for scolding white people for their failure to properly desire whiteness. In this way, these manifestos reflect the rhetorical norms of /pol/'s ecology.

Illustrative of this novel argumentation style, many assailants characterize whiteness as moribund and impotent. For example, the Christchurch shooter writes: "If there is one thing I want you to remember from these writings, its [*sic*] that the birthrates must change. Even if we were to deport all Non-Europeans from our lands tomorrow, the European people would still be spiraling into decay and eventual death. Every day we become fewer in number, we grow older, we grow weaker. In the end we must return to replacement fertility levels, or it will kill us."[42] Although such sexual fears of dark-skinned bodies are well rehearsed, here the trope is turned on its head by a representation of whiteness as inferior, frail, and impotent. As this passage exemplifies, for white nationalists on /pol/, the global border and immigration crisis is the byproduct of white people's insufficient investment in whiteness and racial purity. The figure of the bourgeois Malthusian couple referenced herein, once praised by demographers and population scientists for practicing child-spacing and using appropriate methods of birth control, is summoned not as an index of racial superiority but instead as the failure of white desire. Taking direct inspiration from the Christchurch shooter, the Buffalo assailant also characterized traditional white heterosexuality as "failing," claiming that "white people are failing to reproduce, failing to create families, failing to have children. But despite this sub-replacement fertility rate, the population in the West is increasing rapidly."[43] Ironically, white moral and sexual restraint—traits once described by scientific racists as a byproduct of their physical and intellectual superiority—are reframed as tokens of weakness. In likening individualism to an affliction or disease, the Christchurch and Buffalo assailants echo early twentieth-century discourse about "racial suicide," when low white birthrates were both a masculine and racial concern. In this discourse, psychosomatic and wholly fabricated disorders, such as neurasthensia, named the sapping of manly energies caused by an overcivilized Victorian culture.[44] Similarly, for these assailants, whiteness has lost its manly potency as the result of an indulgence in self-interest over collective racial health. Thus, they characterize Western civilization as a dying culture doomed by its overweening commitment to individualism.

White terrorist manifestos berate Western democracies for the corruption of whiteness by secularism and cultural decadence, which portend the toppling of traditional structures of authority.[45] In a number of passages, the authors link individualism with moral decay, hedonism, and the replacement of God with consumerism. For instance, the Buffalo assailant argues that his intent is "to add momentum to the pendulum swings of history, further destabilizing and polarizing Western society in order to eventually destroy the current nihilistic, hedonistic, individualistic insanity that has taken control of Western thought."[46] The El Paso shooter also adds his affinity for "even the Americans that seem hell-bent on destroying our country. Even if they are shameless race mixers, massive polluters, haters of our collective values, etc. One day they will see the error of their ways."[47] Presumably his expressive content would help his fellow whites to see the error of their race-mixing ways. In explaining the proximate causes of white genocide, the Christchurch shooter observes that "there are myriad reasons behind the decline in fertility rates and the destruction of the traditional family unit. We must inevitably correct the disaster of hedonistic, nihilistic individualism."[48] In other words, transformations in the white family portend the erosion of other transcendent and collective symbols of social authority, ranging from the family, the church, and the state, among others. This moral decay and nihilism signal weakness, a decline in virility that invites aggression from high-fertility cultures.

In making their case for fascist principles, many assailants asserts that immigrants and other hostile foreign enemies seek to exploit waning white racial identification and appreciation for racial heritage. Hence, the assailants charge that white people must radically reconsider their failed investments in whiteness if they are to contain a mobile racial threat. For example, the Christchurch shooter notes that "they [immigrants] see the decay all around them, plummeting, free-falling birth rates all across the Western world. Millions of invaders landing on our shores, conquering our towns and without a single shot fired in response. Broken families with soaring divorce rates, that's if they even bother to get married at all."[49] The Poway Synagogue assailant singles out Jews as particularly opportunist and blames them for promoting hedonist values and "for their role in feminism which has enslaved women in sin; for causing many to fall into sin with their role in peddling pornography" and "for promoting race mixing."[50] In these passages, the authors suggest a series of causal relationships between falling white birthrates and a well-orchestrated set of foreign conspiracies designed to destabilize the traditional nuclear family. In doing so, the assailants project intention and personal motives onto demographic, religious, and consumer trends that have no inherent or necessary connection. The inputting of nefarious motive onto impersonal sociological forces, attributing design to happenstance, recasts violence against civilian noncombatants as armed enemy forces hiding in plain sight. Thus, the supposed decline of traditional Western values is not cultural *suicide*, but instead, *genocide*. Pornography, consumerism, women's liberation, and sexual freedom are reframed as part of intimate guerrilla warfare being perpetrated on an endangered white minority.

Most importantly, many assailants blame the amorality underlying late capitalism for the decline in white racial identification. This claim underwrites the demand politics of each manifesto; namely, a demand to reinstitute race as a meaning-making system. In a particularly illustrative passage, the Christchurch shooter posits that consumerism had supplanted race and religion as the metaphysical guarantors of the symbolic order. He writes that "The truth is that the West killed the notion of god, and proceeded to replace it with nothing. Brought forth two competing ideologies (communism and fascism) to replace this loss of god, then proceeded to allow both sides to laugh at each other to a standstill and then let corporate backed capitalists tear the survivor to pieces. Resulting in a society with no core beliefs, no purpose and no vision for the future. A society of rampant nihilism, consumerism and individualism, where every individual is a competitor and the rights of the individual override all notions of responsibility. In this hell the individual is all and the race is worthless, something to rail against and use whenever possible, a power structure to climb, or topple."[51] Though it might be tempting to read this passage as a call for the return of traditional moral and religious conservatism, the context and source material for this argument suggest that it is instead a demand for the return of the Law, or what Lacan called the symbolic father. In this passage, the demand for God expresses an underlying yearning for unicity and metaphysical backing for white racial identity. This is not so much a lecture on family values as much as it is a demand for the return of the paternal function of the signifier, or in Lacan's words, "The original representative of the Law's authority."[52] The symbolic father is neither a real person nor an idealized ego image but a function of signification, the final and legislative "no" that reminds individuals that no one is above the Law.[53] Here, the problem with individualism, secularism, and consumerism is that each chips away at the presumed ontological authority of racial signifiers. For many of the assailants, individualism prevents whites from thinking in and through the structures of white collective identity—found most prominently in political ideologies that demand authoritarian power structures (fascism, ethnonationalism). In these systems, complete subjects are those who possess a strong sense of racial identification and identification with paternal authority. Contrary to critical racial scholarship, which points to how possessive individualism implicitly conflates freedom with whiteness and masculinity, the assailants argue that the problem of individualism is that it is not *sufficiently* racialized.[54] In other words, whiteness has been divorced from its metonymic and metaphorical connection to authority, superiority, and humanness. For white terrorists, "white" as a racial signifier has lost its "symbolic efficiency" in a postracial world.[55]

Contextually, these manuscripts exemplify how far-right digital ecologies strongly diverge from traditional or neoconservative ideology, particularly in their explicit investment in racial consciousness. Whereas mainstream and public-facing conservatives invest in a colorblind conviction that Western democratic values and modes of government are uniquely superior and should therefore be aggressively promoted abroad, white nationalists adopt a more pessimistic view toward modernity that some have dubbed the "dark enlightenment," or NeoReaction (NRx).[56] Users of 4chan/pol/ embrace antiliberal and antihumanistic political ideologies, including those that promote the acceleration of capitalism to induce economic and geopolitical crises and usher in a transition to new fascist modes of government. In fact, despite their embrace of far-right ideology, the El Paso, Poway, Buffalo, and Christchurch assailants all explicitly repudiate Trump and the GOP as emissaries of crony capitalism. Specifically, as the El Paso assailant puts it, "America is rotting from the inside out, and peaceful means to stop this seem to be nearly impossible. The inconvenient truth is that our leaders, both Democrat AND Republican, have been failing us for decades. They are either complacent or involved in one of the biggest betrayals of the American public in our history."[57]

Hence, these manifestoes are littered with references to fomenting geopolitical divisions, attacking both liberal and conservative belief systems, and exasperating existing cultural tensions to the point of crisis, particularly in the United States (we address these issues in greater detail in chapter 3). One of the reasons the Christchurch shooter lists for carrying out his attack is "to create conflict between the two ideologies within the United States on the ownership of firearms in order to further the social, cultural, political and racial divide within the United states."[58] This rhetoric is a far cry from neoconservative mythologies of colorblindness and Western exceptionalism.

Rather than transform and assimilate non-Western people into a culture of generically Western values, white nationalists pursue racial separation and self-determination—a counterintuitive solution they argue would best preserve (white) racial diversity.[59] As a result, the Christchurch assailant explains that "expecting immigrants to assimilate to a dying, decadent culture is laughable. Who would willing [*sic*] leave their own strong, dominant and rising culture to join an elderly, decaying, degenerate culture? What culture would entice a man, one of traditions, beauty, architecture, art and prosperity, or a culture of decay, self-hatred, childlessness, disorder and nihilism?"[60] It would be fair to characterize this position as Europessimism insofar as the Enlightenment principles designed to sustain the white rights-bearing subject are viewed as that subject's undoing. A funhouse mirror image of theories of Afropessimism,[61] white nationalist rhetoric of this sort asserts that Western individualism is bankrupt because it precludes the kind of higher-order racial identifications necessary to full human enfranchisement. Hence, assailants often contrast the image of a decrepit white subject of Western individualism to that of the youthful, vital, and high-fertility immigrant. For instance, the Christchurch shooter imagines immigrants as overflowing with forms of enjoyment precluded by Western culture. In one sense, the author attributes excessive fertility rates to racial and cultural factors, such as "higher social trust and strong, robust traditions that seek to occupy my peoples lands and ethnically replace my own people."[62] Immigrants possess "vitality and vigour,"[63] evidenced by their "healthy culture,"[64] with "high in group preference and a will to conquer."[65] They are so strong, and in fact, "our own people are beginning to join them, looking outside their own watered down and deteriorating culture to look for purpose and guidance from outside sources."[66] He makes a significant distinction between other racial and ethnic groups by suggesting that they "can be dealt with in time, but the high fertility immigrants will destroy us now, soon it is a matter of survival we destroy them [*sic*] first."[67] Although he continually referred to immigrants as invaders, he characterizes their cultural differences as positive virtues, including large families, strong traditions, youthful vigor, in-group solidarity, and the will to power.

The Christchurch assailant's provisional appreciation of non-Western cultures stem from his belief that sexual reproduction is a weapon in a war of attrition. In all their monstrous manifestations, racial others nonetheless enjoy cultural and sexual excesses prohibited by Western individualism.

What is perhaps most perplexing is that, despite their justifications for racist violence, the Christchurch, Buffalo, and El Paso assailants never characterize white Europeans or Western culture as innately superior. In fact, they reserve their worst cultural indictments for white people; namely, their willingness to participate in their own subjugation and sexual humiliation (exemplified by the ubiquitous /pol/ insults, "cuck" and "eurocuck," which reference a genre of racial pornography). Yet, the manifestos couch their otherwise sincere commitments to racial purity in a liberal language of multiculturalism. The Christchurch shooter claims to have carried out his attack in the name of diversity, "to ensure diverse peoples remain diverse, separate, unique, undiluted in unrestrained cultural or ethnic expression and autonomy."[68] The El Paso shooter also notes that he was "against race mixing" but "because it destroys genetic diversity and creates identity problems."[69] Of course, these investments in innate biological differences, fears of miscegenation, and calls to preserve the purity of racial bloodlines always circle back around to fundamental tenets of white supremacy.[70] Hall's sliding signifier and Fanon's phobic object return to disavow the humanness of racial others—the initial and most fundamental construct of racism. Thus, the assailants' appreciation for diversity belies their forceful demand to expel racial impurities. As the Christchurch shooter writes, "in my mind a rainbow is only beautiful to due [*sic*] its variety of colours, mix the colours together and you destroy them all and they are gone forever and the end result is far from anything beautiful."[71] In these passages, the one drop rule of hypodescent resurfaces to dictate that non-white blood sullies and nullifies whiteness in all its pristineness.[72]

For white nationalists, this defense of purity is important for whiteness to continue to serve as a signifier of universal humanity. But unlike colorblind and postracial discourse, the form of racism expressed here foregrounds a kind of racial particularity, or white identity politics, that is foreclosed by the implicit codes of whiteness.[73] Although it would be difficult to confuse these alleged or convicted killers for liberal multiculturalists, their cynical redeployment of diversity speaks to how new forms of racist rhetoric cloak sincere investments in white supremacy with an insincere appreciation for particularity across a spectrum of racial difference. In this case, appreciation quickly veers to anxiety that whiteness will be imperiled by the innate aggression, excessive fertility, and ugliness of racial others. The enjoying Other must be not only expelled but eradicated.

THE WHITE CHILD (IS BEING BEATEN)

The Christchurch, Buffalo, and Bratislava assailants continually ruminate on the overriding imperative of white supremacy: "We must ensure the existence of our people, and a future for White Children [*sic*]."[74] In these manifestos, children bear the symbolic burdens of white futurity. For instance, the Christchurch assailant emphasizes the unique sexual threat faced by white children as metonymy for a kind of molestation or sexual violation of whiteness itself. In one section, the author provides a series of links to Wikipedia pages that detail incident after incident of child sex abuse to document an "ongoing trend of rape and molestation perpetrated by these non-White scum."[75] He continues, "The true number of these events perpetrated across the Western world is unknown and certainly under reported, as both the state, the media and the judicial system work in unison to hide these atrocities, in the fear that knowledge of these events would enrage the native people of the West and damage the perception of our new 'Multicultural utopia.'" He ended the section by demanding, "KILL THE RAPISTS, HANG THEIR FAMILIES."[76] Although the Buffalo assailant copied and pasted this passage (among many others), he also adds his own list of Talmudic passages that suggest that Jews—who he believed were the orchestrators of racial replacement—are charged with a divine mandate to violate white gentile children sexually. For these two assailants, racial pluralists conceal sex abuse not simply because they are embarrassed about the risks immigration poses to white children, but rather because racial pluralism is *itself* a form of sexual violation. In other words, the Christchurch and Buffalo assailants likened whiteness to an endangered white child and molestation as a representative anecdote for the sexual threat of racial otherness.

In several instances, the Christchurch and Buffalo assailants evoke the figure of the endangered white child as a metonym for the sanctity and vulnerability of white identity. For example, the Christchurch assailant ruminates over the death of Ebba Akerlund, a deaf girl struck and killed by a truck during at 2017 terrorist attack in Stockholm, Sweden. "Young, innocent, and dead Ebba" killed "at the hands of the invaders, the indignity of her violent demise and my inability to stop it broke my own jaded cynicism like a sledgehammer."[77] Similarly the Buffalo assailant copied and pasted dozens of infographics and memes pulled directly from /pol/ asserting that Jews are responsible for numerous kidnappings and child murders in the West, as well as the broader global sex trade in children. Both men attribute their own racial consciousness to knowledge of child sex abuse allegedly perpetrated by Jews, Muslims, and people of color. But the threats they articulate have less to do with actual children per se than the idyllic image of white futurity for which they stand.

As enduring icons of innocence and purity, the figure of the yet-to-be realized child reinvests whiteness with vigor, youth, and vitality. The white child underwrites what Lee Edelman calls *reproductive futurism*, a heterosexual fantasy of a symbolic order stabilized by the yet-to-be child and whose namesake purchases "the realization of the subject's authentic presence in the Child imagined as enjoying access to Imaginary wholeness'"[78] Edelman contends that heterosexual sex always concerns the "future of signification," insofar as the future child retroactively installs meaning and coherence into the symbolic.[79] For Edelman, the refusal to procreate is "inherently destructive of meaning and therefore as responsible for the undoing of social organization, collective reality, and, inevitably, life itself."[80] In light of the assailants' concerns with the diminishing symbolic efficiency of whiteness, we might understand their preoccupation with a future for white children as the recuperative counterpart to the enjoying Other. In other words, the child is both a traumatic reminder of the subject's sacrifice into language and its imagined fulfillment prior thereof, as white reproductive futurity constitutes a racialized fantasy of gratification brought about by an encounter with whiteness as a stand-in for wholeness and coherence. Hence, the Christchurch assailant imagines "a [white] nation that venerates its ancestors, but lives for its offspring."[81] The fantasy keeps at bay the recognition that whiteness is simply a signifier like any other with no inherent or transcendent value outside of language.

If we take the assailants to mean that individualism has quelled the physical drive to reproduce and that multiculturalism has eradicated racial collectivism, whiteness under Western liberalism is ostensibly queer in its refusal to both physically and symbolically procreate. This queer, childless caricature of whiteness is not simply an amplification of earlier arguments about nihilism and cultural decadence, but also a portrait of white identity as "intransigent jouissance, by figuring sexuality's implication in the senseless compulsions of that drive."[82] The Christchurch assailant presents whiteness as unmoored from the productive engine of self-realization and desire that reproduces "white" as a signifier. In this regard, the manifesto chains a fantasy of traumatic white identity that must continually seek its own renewal and infuse the symbolic with its meaning. As the assailant emphatically repeated, "WITHOUT CHILDREN, THERE IS NO FUTURE."[83]

The unicity of the white child stands in relation to the disorder wrought by children of so-called "vipers," for whom he unequivocally prescribes violent eradication.[84] He explains, "Any invader you kill, of any age, is one less enemy your children will have to face."[85] Hence, the refusal to have (white) children or see reproduction as central to the meaning of white identity constitutes a refusal of racial order. The white child and its imperilment stand in as an enjoying other—not one that must be eradicated out of envy but instead one that must be recovered so that its imagined wholeness can be enjoyed.

Ironically, the construction of the white child as a figure in perpetual danger is central to the racial investments and queer disavowals entailed by white futurity. The Christchurch and Buffalo assailants' continual ruminations on pedophilia and child sex abuse supposedly perpetrated by both Muslim immigrants and white perverts are, to be sure, convenient warrants for violence against the superlative evil attributed to sexual predators and deviants. In another sense, the accompanying figure of the pedophile stands in for a perversion of whiteness, a kind of queer and deviant misfiring of proper libidinal investments. Hence, the Christchurch shooter insists:

> Pedophile politicians, pedophile priests and pedophile pop stars, demonstrating to all the true depravity of our age. Art and beauty subverted beyond all recognition, bauhaus travesties replacing nouveau wonders, soulless metropolitan architecture of glass and steel reflecting no society, no culture, no people and therefore belonging everywhere, and no where. Suicidal, nihilistic and degenerate pop icons produced from a dead culture: Michael Jackson (pedophile, self hating, self mutilating, opioid addict); Madonna (degenerate, drug addict, childless, whore, anti-christian, pro miscegenation) Kurt Cobain(suicidal, drug addict, self hater, antisocial), Freddy Mercury (lifelong identity crisis, lifelong battle with hedonism and drug use, eventual death due to sexual hedonism) just to name a few. Empty nurseries, full casinos, empty churches and full mosques, entropy in blitzspeed. Politicians write in the same ink as Eligabolus, worshiping all that is foreign, poisonous and subversive.[86]

In this passage, the ubiquity of pedophiles, addicts, and perverts signals a broader divestment from white identity and institutions. The pedophile indexes a cultural failure to sublimate the drives in the name of civilizational progress. The disavowal at work here relies not only on a sedimented homophobic mythology of the queer sex predator, but also the entanglement of whiteness and reproductive futurism. In other words, the pedophile is a race traitor insofar as he refuses to sublimate their desires to the reproduction and sanctity of the white child.

Finally, both the Christchurch and Buffalo manifesto conclude with a series of eight images of white families and children. The images vary in resolution and appear to be pulled from a cross section of advertisements and stock photos available on a Google image search. The photos in the Christchurch manifesto are arranged two by four and are held together by an overlapping pagan symbol, the Schwarze Sonne (Black Sun), most commonly associated with the

Nazi SS and the occult preoccupations of Nazi leader Heinrich Himmler. According to the Southern Poverty Law Center's catalog of far-right symbols, the Black Sun has been adopted by white supremacists groups to signify a mythical form of whiteness rooted in pre-European Norse and Germanic tribes.[87] Three images feature women tending to young children, two images feature men in full paramilitary garb displaying heavy armaments, two images show men camping or exploring pristine wilderness, and the last image on the bottom right features a father and son sharing a caring moment on a lush bluff overlooking the ocean. Without captions of explanation, the images create a tableau of white futurity that represent the manifestos' racial and gender investments.

These images offer an idyllic portrait of the traditional white family and its close ties to bucolic rural life. The images of women caring for young children convey both white innocence and fragility in that the protection of women and children is always articulated as the task of white civilization. Indeed, these images are accompanied by portraits of white masculinity as militaristic, protective, and tied to the land—a passing homage to the Nazi battle cry "blut and boden" ("blood and soil"). But, aside from presenting a wistful vision of white separatism, the images also reflect a ritual purification of whiteness that is enacted through public murder. That is to say, the images are central to the manifestos' conflation of whiteness with completeness, something only achieved through racial violence as represented by the presence of the gun. Pedophilia stands in for the perversion and sexual victimization of whiteness enacted by ceaseless reproduction of racial others. These images constitute a cathexis or libidinal investment in whiteness; both sex and violence should be seen as essential components of a white racial consciousness, much in the same way that lynching cements connections between eroticism, white citizenship, and racist violence. The innocent white child is not simply a rallying cry but an object that stands in place of the imagined wholeness and purity of whiteness itself. To put it crassly, this new youthful vitality is only possible if whites are willing to kill and fuck for their race. Such manifestos invite their audience to infuse the symbolic with the codes of white race consciousness.

THE CODES OF OVERT RACISM

Thomas K. Nakayama makes the observation that "whiteness is not contained."[88] That is to say, whiteness does not abide by our prescribed rules and grids of intelligibility. Just as we think we have mapped its terrain and named it structural operations, whiteness shifts its topography, evades and absorbs threats, and consternates its critics. Whiteness does not respect boundaries and borders. Myra Washington compares whiteness to a road. She writes that critical race scholars find "the road they are traveling has changed, or moved, maybe added a toll, so the journey to reach the destination is different, possibly difficult, maybe even treacherous."[89] The investments do not change; they simply become more opaque. We find that the overt racism of this particular historical moment to be no exception. In one sense, these manifestos are vile screeds devoid of the elegant disavowals and nimble colorblind rhetoric that critical race scholars have become adept at deciphering. In another sense, even in their bald effacement of people of color and perverse ownership of overt racism, the manifestos set out to stabilize white identity. These manifestos illustrate how the codes of overt white supremacy reterritorialize and build affective investments in white identity to reckon with its impending demographic decline.

Nakayama also notes that even as whiteness remains evasive and diffuse, nonetheless, "whiteness has been among the most stable identity terms, a reflection of its place in the racial hierarchy."[90] Thus, even as white nationalists fret over conspiracies and demographic crisis, white as a signifier has not lessened in symbolic value, for as long as race exists as a prism through which we comprehend difference there always remains a residue of the racist investments that went into the crafting of the concept. It is for this reason that Hall argues that, even as the biological discourse of race is "shown out the front door," it "tends to sidle around the edge of the veranda and climb back in through the pantry window!"[91] Race is always retains a standing tropological reserve and an imaginary that continually sutures whiteness to whatever it needs to be at a particular moment. The manifestos we have analyzed in this chapter attempt to stabilize whiteness not through outright proclamations of its own supremacy but rather by attaching itself to weakness, pessimism, and victimhood. In doing so, white identity shuttles back and forth between racial universality to particularity. Whiteness is both a stand in for humanity and a specific identity category deserving of the same protections as any other. Although whites will cease to be a majority in the US, they enjoy an abundance of material and symbolic wealth. Although the era of postracialism evacuated public life of racial conversations that were threatening to white privilege, it left a void filled by fragile and reactionary voices.

The rhetoric of replacement is, among many things, a reframing of white terrorism as collective self-defense. In imagining themselves as the victims rather than the perpetrators of genocide, whites disown their own genocidal legacy and justify future acts of white violence. In an argument that strains the limits of incredulity, whiteness transforms into sexual and racial vulnerability. The amalgam that is the world's Black and Brown populations threaten to overwhelm the white world with their exponential rates of reproduction and their unified racial consciousness as weapons in a demographic war of attrition. Fanon observed that white hysteria—its preoccupation with the excessive fertility of nonwhites—ironically anchored white identity as much to what it was (humanity) than what it was not (abject). Given the explicit exclusion of nonwhite populations from Enlightenment concepts of personhood, the "self" in "self-defense" is always already white.[92] Thus, even as white phobias take on the characteristics of the absurd, they are nonetheless coherent with the broader rhetorics of whiteness that help fashion for Whites an innocent and vulnerable identity.

We have turned to the psychoanalytical work of Fanon and Lacan to make sense of the sexual and racial investments of white supremacy. Our objective in this chapter was to frame the rhetoric of replacement as an erotic fantasy to be disavowed through acts of violence. Central to white supremacy is the figure of an *enjoying Other*, a subject who experiences an unmediated encounter with the completeness and unicity experienced prior to its nullification by the entry into language. The enjoying Other takes on a number of forms. At some points, the enjoying other is a figure whose primitive sexual capacities threaten to overwhelm white civilization. Here the body of the Other is, ontologically speaking, a weapon. At other points, the enjoying Other takes the form of the white child, whose recovery in the name of futurity stages an encounter with an unadulterated form of wholeness that redeems and sanctifies white identity. Either way, the enjoying Other hinges on sexualized racism in which the white subject externalizes his own desires onto others. In specific historical terms, white killers imagine a racial Other caught up in the unfettered experience of *jouissance*. The hypersexuality of the racial Other can, thus, only be avenged through violence. The manifestos imagine this Other as gaining power through its sexual dominance—casting white violence as the fulfillment of a rape revenge cycle similar to the ritual of lynching. But this fear is not isolated to paranoid white men enraptured and caught up in the nets of signifiers that constitute the confounding and unstable world of online white supremacy. The fear that a demographic shift may shift the balance of power is latently sexual in that reproduction is a route to racial dominance. More importantly, however, is that a demographic shift will undermine white as a signifier of both universal humanness and moral superiority. The white genocide manifesto installs racial others as barriers to white people enjoying their subjectivity. In this regard, the enjoying Other is anathema to white futurity and, thus, the likely inspiration for future mass violence.

2

Antiheroism and Necroempowerment

THE CHRISTCHURCH KILLER's call to arms implored his fellow partisans to "accept death" and "embrace infamy." For killers like himself, "the media will paint you as villains, the state will name you as traitors, the globalist forces will name you as criminals and the traitors amongst your people will name you as enemies. You will be infamous until victory is achieved. Take it with a smile. ACCEPT DEATH, EMBRACE INFAMY, ACHIEVE VICTORY."[1] Although such an injunction may seem obscene or counterintuitive, it exemplifies the tropology of violence that white men have historically called upon to legitimize and recodify their sovereign authority in the face of perceived challenges.[2] As historian Richard Slotkin illustrates, the trope of "regeneration through violence" names a pattern of settler colonial discourse in which genocide and mass slaughter of indigenous people was authorized by the metaphysical association of such acts with signifiers of rebirth, renewal, and revitalization of Western civilization.[3] Whereas the previous chapter explored the racist and sexual tropology of mass killers, this chapter attends to the supporting cast of tropes that glorify violence, death, and revenge. For so-called aggrieved white men, the "appeal" of embracing something like naked violence and villainy is that such behaviors dethrone democratic rules, conventions, and taboos that have constrained and frustrated white men's ability to recuperate their perceived loss of unassailable social, economic, and political status. Indeed, public murder turns the world upside down. As such, white terrorist manifestos present killing as an honorable act of rebellion against a feminized culture of decadence and amorality, much like the ethos of *Fight Club*'s fictional Project Mayhem.[4] These texts seek not only to legitimize defensive violence against threatening "invaders," but also to glorify the act of killing as a genre of white masculine empowerment.

In a broader context, such perverse statements are consistent with what Slavoj Žižek and Jodi Dean, among others, have identified as the steady decline in "symbolic efficiency" in the West, naming the coalescence of a broad distrust in traditional signifiers of authority and expertise, exemplified by conspiratorial and paranoid reading practices, but also a general disdain for the rules and conventions that organize the social and psychic existence of subjects in democratic cultures.[5] As Joshua Gunn observes, one consequence of the decline in symbolic efficiency has been a widespread embrace of the *perverse*, meaning that communicative practices have shifted away from those that structure adherence to consensus reality—governed by norms and conventions—toward a dystopian social imaginary in which subjects are habituated to enjoying obscene transgression against cultural prohibitions, violence included.[6] According to Gunn, perversity entails speech and forms of representation that simultaneously acknowledge and disavow symbolic authority ("I know it's wrong, but I'm going to do it anyway"). Such rebellions are now quotidian—the ironic viewing practices of reality television, former President Trump's routine flaunting of legal and social norms, unhinged conspiracy theories espoused by QAnon, entertainment featuring empathetic serial killers, or even something as mundane as a tongue-in-cheek dorm room poster featuring the mug shot of *narco cultura* kingpin Pablo Escobar.

In this chapter, we read these manifestos as part of a broader pattern of speech and expressive conduct in US media culture that disinhibits white masculine violence and embraces the trope of the antihero. Indeed, US media culture, too, has "accepted death" and "embraced infamy" in and through its construction of compelling narratives and backstories for violent male antiheroes, such as Walter White, Tony Soprano, Dexter Morgan, Jax Teller, Marty Byrde, and Stringer Bell, just to name a few.[7] What these characters share in common is a turn toward violence and illicit markets as alternative channels for personal empowerment and financial gain that require the acceptance, if not glorification, of (self-defensive) violence and death. Antiheroes are "character[s] who [are] our primary point of ongoing narrative alignment but whose behavior and beliefs provoke ambiguous, conflicted, or negative moral allegiance."[8] According to Yael Levy, "the antihero's journey is associated with introducing moral disorder to the social order."[9] The ubiquity of antiheroes reflects the decoupling of white masculinity with traditional signifiers of authority as well as the kind of economic mobility that has by and large evaporated over the neoliberal period. Since the 1980s, neoliberal deregulation schemes have undone the models of labor and liberal governance that once secured "the good life" for white men who demonstrated adherence to principles of being responsible, self-reliant, hard working, and engaging in private initiative.[10] As Jack Bratich and Sarah Banet-Weiser point out, the failure of neoliberalism to deliver on this promise has eroded its capacity to secure white men within its political subjectivity.[11] In response to this failure, white men have displaced blame onto women, immigrants, people of color, and other minoritized groups. Some have turned to public murder as a means to resecure what neoliberal capitalism could never ultimately deliver to them.[12] Much like the antihero, the white terrorist reflects white men's failure to embody traditional models of paternal authority and, consequently, a desire to recuperate moral authority outside of the boundaries of the law and propriety.

It should come as no surprise, then, that real-life killers would construct themselves and their acolytes in a similar manner: as ordinary guys who turn to crime and violence as an alternative form of empowerment. Sayak Valencia traces this fascination with violent antiheroes—serial killers, *narcos*, *sicarios*, mafiosos, hitmen, mercenaries, kingpins, mass shooters, and other "violence specialists"—to the emergence of *gore capitalism*, or what she defines as the latest phase of capitalism in which death, killing, and maiming have become forms of capital accumulation, entertainment, and empowerment.[13] She writes that "the production of dead, mutilated, brutalized bodies becomes a kind of commodity that maintains and *justifies itself* according to the supply-and-demand logics of the new capitalism."[14] Gore capitalism offers an alternative model of primitive accumulation that increasingly expands the parameters of the precariat while spectralizing and glorifying the violence this process necessarily entails. As precarious populations find themselves immobilized, destitute, and with ostensibly nothing left to lose, the drive for advancement is sublimated into illicit markets and violent forms of entrepreneurialism.[15] Popular culture's celebration of antiheroes is just one symptom of an emergent form of neoliberal capitalism in which violence is celebrated, or at the very least tolerated, as a genre of masculine empowerment.

As such, white terrorists have begun to construct themselves as outlaws, partisans, guerrilla warriors, or rebels left with no other option but to kill for racial supremacy and economic advancement. Their manifestos blame corporate exploitation of cheap immigrant labor ("invaders") for displacing the traditional pathways to economic success that once guaranteed white men a chance at achieving the good life. According to these killers, the replacement of the white worker with people of color is an economic scheme so vast and powerful that it can only be upended through public murder. Of course, these assailants did not need much assistance in disinhibiting violent impulses, given that the digital ecologies in which they honed their theories were already saturated with derealized violence, including pro-Nazi memes, genocide jokes, serial killer fandom, suicide and death videos, violent pornography and snuff films, gory images, and other abominable content.[16] In fact, there are entire Tumblr "true crime" communities devoted to fandom of mass murderers from Ted Bundy to the Columbine High School shooters.[17] The white terrorist stands at the confluence of the declining respect for democratic norms, waning of producerist white masculinity, resurgent nativism, and the capitalistic glorification of gore. White terrorists are entrepreneurs of death, opportunistically killing and maiming in the gore marketplace to disrupt other racial groups competing for the same opportunities as whites. The embrace of death and infamy represent a kind of perversion that Valencia calls "thanatophilia," which simply names the "predilection for the spectacularization of death in contemporary hyperconsumerist societies, as well as the taste for violence and destruction, its desire to kill, and its attraction to suicide and sadism."[18] Yet, in the guise of anticapitalist rebellion, white terrorists take the neoliberal credo of "creative destruction" and its directives about personal responsibility to their ultimate though logical conclusion.[19]

This chapter examines how replacement rhetoric advances tropes of antiheroism and necroempowerment, a process whereby subjects of late capitalism turn to the infliction of death and maiming as forms of agency and value. In doing so, these killers perform the role of the antihero, a figure who hastens the depreciation of traditional authority and the public good that once guaranteed "the good life" to white men in favor of a feral "disinhibited freedom" unyoked from moral considerations save the preservation of white life. They are, in Wendy Brown's words, "humanity without a project other than revenge."[20] Indeed, much like the hyperconsumerist society they reject, mass shooters invite audiences to refuse the most basic democratic and moral injunctions against instrumental violence and instead, in the words of the Christchurch assailant, "accept death" and "embrace infamy." Their manifestos go well beyond excusing defensive violence by glorifying death and self-destruction in a manner consistent with the ontology of gore capitalism. Although these killers make threat calculations that seemingly exempt their violence from moral sanction, their rhetoric more directly ennobles killing in the name of white racial advancement. White terrorists go to great lengths, then, to minimize the significance of individual lives, their own lives included, relative to population-level survival. The only thing that gives individual lives any value beyond their whiteness—economic or otherwise—is the glory of their sacrifice. That is to say, the will to power that is required to turn their lives into an instrument of death, sacrificing others as well as themselves for the greater good of saving white lives, is ultimately what makes any individual life grievable.

WE COULD BE (ANTI)HEROES

White terrorist manifestoes construct the persona of the mass shooter as a white antihero, detailing his transition from meek and lawful conformist to morally dubious though sympathetic outlaw. One recurring argument across these manifestos is that white European men have allowed themselves to be emasculated by the creature comforts of late capitalism and henpecked by the diversity credos of modern democracy. Yet, in the Christchurch shooter's words, "The people who are to blame most are ourselves, european [*sic*] men. Strong men do not get ethnically replaced, strong men do not allow their culture to degrade, strong men do not allow their people to die. Weak men have created this situation and strong men are needed to fix it."[21] This portrait of white masculinity in crisis maps onto the life of pop culture antiheroes prior to their transformation into hypermasculine outlaws: they start out as ineffectual, nihilistic, passive, dispossessed, and complacent. This image also bears a strong resemblance to other anticonsumerist discourses in the West that lament the phoniness and femininity of the mass culture that has supplanted the authenticity and dignity of the masculine producerist work ethic.[22] The key difference, however, is that the assailants locate masculine agency not in theories of possessive individualism, but rather in collective racial identification and primal violence. The problem, the assailants surmise, is that unlike other racial groups, white men have been compelled to inhibit their natural impulses toward traditional authority, dominance, and violence.

Although the Christchurch assailant also blames consumerism and cheap immigrant labor for destroying traditional values and "ethnic autonomy," his manifesto is preoccupied with strength and virility—idealizing masculine bodies steeled and capacitated by their willingness to sacrifice a comfortable life ("nihilism, consumerism, and individualism") for collective survival. According to his reasoning, strong men do not permit foreigners to dictate the direction of the culture, nor do they cede their future aspirations to lesser men.[23] By contrast, "invaders" are able to replace "native" whites precisely because multicultural democracy permits them to retain cultural and religious traditions that privilege the Other's masculine authority. White men, on the other hand, are victims of *overcivilization*.[24] Thus, he proclaimed that white men "are expected not to combat these myriad, unending and dedicated interlopers, but to embrace them, accept their own disenfranchisement, accept the loss of their fathers lands, their own impoverishment, their own REPLACEMENT."[25] The solution, then, is for white men to disinhibit those violent and authoritarian impulses that have been repressed in the name of multicultural democracy, or for the "Men of the West" to become "men once more."[26] It is not coincidence that the manifesto concludes with a series of images of men in pristine wilderness, dressed in paramilitary garb and carrying automatic weapons. Although one day they may be celebrated as avenging heroes, for now they must embrace their role as villains to even the score.

Although the assailants' defense of committing atrocities mirrors many of the same historical justifications for lynching[27]—that is, it is considered a "heroic" extralegal protection of white women and children—contemporary white terrorists lean more heavily on tropes of antiheroism insofar they propose and enact a system of morality that would be reprehensible to most audiences. Yet, despite their perverse moral beliefs, they find their own personas and backstories so compelling that they deserve pages of elaborate explanation and appreciation. For instance, the Christchurch assailant's use of an extended hypothetical question-and-answer format to convey the underlying justifications for his attack (a practice copied by subsequent killers) implies a hypothetical auditor who is somehow riveted by perverse statements about the inferiority of other races and the need to exterminate civilians, children included, to ensure white survival. In his own words, killing children is "distasteful, it will be damaging to the soul, but know that it is necessary and any invader you spare, no matter the age, will one day be an enemy your people must face. Better for you to face them now then your kin to face them in the future."[28] The El Paso shooter also defended killing innocent civilians by arguing that "it is not cowardly to pick low hanging fruit."[29] Whereas conventional heroism tends to be marked by characteristics like courage, high-minded idealism, and clear moral polarities, antiheroism introduces moral disorder by inverting both common sense and civic virtue. For these assailants, killing is courageous, a child is an acceptable military target, and fascism is freedom, at least for them. They imagine an audience that is somehow morally conflicted, yet compelled by the killer's willingness to violate the most basic cultural prohibitions that we all must live by, in the name of a greater cause.

This is not to suggest that mass killers embrace passive nihilism; rather, they endorse a perverse ethical system that expands the parameters of acceptable violence. As for antiheroes, for mass killers the ends justify the means. As such, unheroic, unredeemable, and barbaric acts are permissible if they are done in the name of white survival. At the same time, mass killer manifestos also illustrate Hannah Arendt's argument that political violence has ceased to be solely instrumental or strategic, meaning that violence is now an end in itself. In other words, the justification for political violence since the twentieth century have become rooted in appeals to the iron laws of nature and history, rather than by necessity alone.[30] Indeed, the Christchurch killer justifies his violence in precisely such terms: "There is no nation in the world that wasn't founded by, or maintained by, the use of force. Force is power. History is the history of power. Violence is power and violence is the reality of history. Wake up."[31] The mass killer as antihero is a figural manifestation of this tautological credo: he uses violence as both an instrumental and categorical imperative. Put another way, violence is a historical and natural fact that justifies white supremacy but the historical fact of white supremacy also justifies violence. As *anti*heroes, then, mass killers are less constrained by the artificial moral prohibitions against violence nor by liberal frameworks of personhood that have grown more capacious, at least in a nominal sense, in response to movements for racial justice and equality. These assailants redefine "courage" as the willingness to embrace their violent nature—violence that even traditional tragic heroes engaging in instrumental actions, such as self-defense or self-sacrifice, would find unimaginable.[32] However, as the Poway Synagogue shooter puts it, it is not killing that is unlawful. Instead, "it is unlawful and cowardly to stand on the sidelines as the European people are genocided [*sic*] around you. I did not want to have to kill Jews. But they have given us no other option."[33]

Many killers admit that their only worthwhile trait is that they are willing to break taboos against violence—to indulge in atavistic fantasies of primal masculine violence. They gild their violence in virtuous populist aphorisms, such as "regular," "simple," and "normal," words that help recast killing as an enactment of common sense in the name of "the people."[34] Populist antiheroes are "courageous" simply because they have accepted violence as both politically efficacious and an unavoidable aspect of the human condition. Indeed, many antiheroes proudly admit that they possess no special traits or extraordinary skills, but simply a willingness to violate top-down moral and legal prohibitions, including actions so terrible that they are barred under international law for use during warfare (i.e., targeting civilian populations). For instance, the Christchurch shooter notes that he is "just a regular White man, from a regular family. Who decided to take a stand to ensure a future for my people."[35] Similarly, the Poway Synagogue assailant proclaims that "I'm just a normal dude who wanted to have a family, help and heal people, and play piano."[36] Killing civilians, however, is not a choice, but rather "the Jew has forced our hand, and our response is completely justified. My God does not take kindly to the destruction of His creation. Especially one of the most beautiful, intelligent, and innovative races that He has created."[37] The El Paso shooter also reiterates this sentiment, claiming "I am simply defending my country from cultural and ethnic replacement brought on by an invasion."[38] The Buffalo assailant similarly claims that "The truth is my personal life and experiences are of no value. I am simply a White man seeking to protect and serve my community, my people, my culture, and my race." He even explains that antiheroism requires an acceptance of death and murder, because it is "very difficult for a normal person even with all the information to carry out an attack that will kill another human being, or the fact that you may die that day."[39] Presumably, only strong men are capable of such radical transgressions.

The "ethics" of white terrorism that emerge from these texts, then, are premised on identification with the morality of necessity but also the sadistic enjoyment of transgressing cultural prohibitions. Adopting this framework entails fundamentally unheroic actions from "normal" men in the name of collective survival, even so-called "soul damaging" atrocities. For these men, violence is a natural response to incursions against "the people," or a vision of the polity of everyday white folks. These killers suggest that they are simply obeying the iron laws of nature and the virtues of populist reason as opposed to the putatively arbitrary moral dictates of liberal democracy. As a consequence, everyday people who pick up arms are without fault. As the El Paso killer put it, "I see my actions as faultless. Because this isn't an act of imperialism but an act of preservation."[40] In defending the morally indefensible, but in the name of common sense, these assailants chip away at the traditional signifiers of heroism. That is to say, conventional conceptions of heroism require a distinction between instrumental and indiscriminate or sadistic violence. But it is the so-called everydayness of these antiheroes that renders indiscriminate killing quotidian and rational: a necessary yet unsavory job that someone has to do.

A SOLDIER'S DEATH

As much as these killers ruminate on the failed state of white masculinity, they optimistically embrace paramilitarism as a mode of transformation and empowerment. Each manifesto includes lengthy details of their armaments, replete with sufficient technological jargon and expert firearms knowledge to signal their embeddedness in gun culture, particularly as it has flourished in digital spaces. For instance, the Bratislava attacker thanked his comrades on "terrorgram"—a series of encrypted channels on the app Telegram devoted to homemade bombs and weapons—for teaching him about advanced weaponry and military tactics. Modeling the style of posts on the weapons image board 4chan/k/, the Buffalo killer devoted dozens of pages to product reviews of guns, tactical gear, body armor, and outdoor survival paraphernalia. The Umpqua Community College killer even critiqued other mass shooters for their low "death tolls," observing that they were not properly trained to kill quickly and with precision.[41] The El Paso shooter coldly weighed the relative advantages and disadvantages of AR-15s versus AK-47s for use against civilian targets. In chapter 4, we take up the anesthetizing function of this paramilitary discourse in great detail. Here, our primary concern is the degree to which these assailants interpret demographic changes as warfare. These manifestos obliterate vital democratic distinctions between the civilian and military contexts of acceptable violence. In doing so, they venerate the soldier as the ideal citizen-subject. An important difference from conventional pro-military hero valorization is the degree to which these assailants apply gore epistemologies and military logics to the challenges of governing in a society marked by democratic pluralism. Moreover, these manifestos lionize soldiers' use of violence in civilian contexts, rather than their sacrifice for the civilian good. By not walling off military and civilian roles, they offer a thanatopolitical framework of governance—a biopolitics of death—that glorifies military violence in civilian life, including killing and suicide in the name of extending white life.[42]

Soldiers are not born; rather, they are constituted through patterns of regimentation and brutalization that prepare subjects to be disciplined, obey orders, maim, and kill.[43] The process of becoming a soldier entails adherence to top-down authority structures and disinhibiting violent impulses that would be unacceptable in civilian life. The use of both targeted and indiscriminate violence against civilian populations has long been prohibited, but they are seldom punished under national and international law. The saturation bombing of Dresden in World War II, the My Lai massacre, the US invasion of Iraq, and the Russian invasion of Ukraine are just a few high-profile incidents of atrocities committed against civilian noncombatants. It is important to note that the soldier constructed in white terrorist manifestos is not a moral entrepreneur but a war criminal and genocidaire, an illicit figure who commits anticivilian violence and who sees the mere existence of the Other as a military threat that must be extinguished. It is this logic that permitted the Christchurch shooter to interpret children as legitimate military targets: "A[n] ounce of prevention is worth a pound of cure. Preventing these enemies from reaching adulthood and their full potential of effect is of the importance. Why make your children fight, when you could fight in their stead?"[44] Characterizing child murder as medicinal encapsulates the misappropriation of military logics to social antagonisms in civilian contexts. Such logics have been used elsewhere to justify the use of "ethnic cleansing" in order to attain social stability and homogeneity by means of war.

How, then, do these assailants glorify the figure of the war criminal? How do they attempt to entice readers to desire a soldier's fight and a soldier's death? What is the lure of paramilitary discourse? Given that many white terrorists were radicalized on Reddit and /pol/, they tend to characterize their own transformation into killers in ways that reflect the traces of digital "Red Pill" discourse, narratives of consciousness raising in which meek men wake up to the reality of their supposed subjugation by feminist and multicultural brainwashing.[45] In doing so, they detail how white men dehumanize themselves, meaning how they exchange attributes such as empathy and compassion for the dispassionate rationalism of the authoritarian personality: they embrace aggression, toughness, destructiveness, and cynicism.[46] In this narrative, the social terrain has already been invaded and colonized by an occupying force. White men have been subjected to decades of egalitarian propaganda designed by the enemy to win the war without having to fire a shot.

Many so-called Red Pill men characterize themselves as edgy countercultural outlaws, charismatic villains, and guerrilla warriors who resist what masquerades as common sense by openly embracing hypermasculinity and white authoritarian heteropatriarchy (sometimes called "white Sharia" law by the extreme far-right).[47] For them, the failure of multicultural democracy is simply an antihero origin story that explains and justifies their turn toward violence. For instance, in the following extended passage, the Christchurch assailant explains how people like himself awoke:

> [They] see this suicidal nihilism and isolate themselves from this mainstream, "multicultural," egalitarian, individualistic insanity and look for allies anywhere they can find them, in the flesh or online. They congregate, discuss, despair, strategize, debate and plan. They decry weakness, mock fecklessness and worship strength, and in this worship of strength they radicalize and find the solution. Somehow this isolation then radicalization is seen as a surprise, yet for anyone who was paying attention, it was a long time coming. . . . People are finding their way home. Finding their people, finding their traditions, seeing through the lies of history, the brainwashing of the institutions and they angry, they are energized and yes, against their degenerate societies, they are radicalized. RADICALIZATION IS THE RATIONAL RESPONSE TO DEGENERATION.[48]

In this excerpt, the author espouses a racist and antifeminist theory of consciousness raising. The West's "suicidal nihilism" and degeneracy drive the strongest and most perceptive among us to peer behind the veil of appearances, sustained by multicultural "brainwashing," to expose the bleak reality that lies beneath. Radicalization unlocks new modes of perception that make gore practices both necessary and desirable. Here, to be an outlaw, a guerrilla warrior, is to be positioned against the hegemonic consensus of the corrupt elite of "degenerate societies," which is ultimately the only rational position one can adopt once they have been introduced to the "desert of the Real."[49]

According to this logic, the mass and serial killer are soldiers in a war over not only terrain but ideas, culture, and bodies. Red Pill discourse primes white men to see war everywhere they turn and to interpret social heterogeneity as a threat to be addressed by militant, if not military means. The only reason "normies" are so reviled by such discourse is because they are conformists who obey their social programming and only accept beliefs that lay within the so-called "Overton window." The Christchurch assailant notes that "The global and corporate ran press controls them, the education system (long since fallen to the long march through the institutions committed by the marxists) controls them, the state (long since heavily lost to its corporate backers) controls them and the anti-white media machine controls them."[50] Here, the author reframes radicalization and militarization as radical consciousness of dangerous truths suppressed to suit the interests of powerful corporations and their progressive allies, or what amounts to an occupying force. Although it is hard to imagine that Marxists and corporations would somehow share an interest in common, the point is to suggest that the intolerant political left will use any strategy necessary, no matter how incoherent or violent, to suppress the harsh truths discovered by those with the courage to ingest the Red Pill.

Thus, these killers and the acolytes they address in their manifestos adopt what Judith Butler calls the "frame of war" to glorify killing and sacrifice as a response to the threat of difference.[51] The frame of war requires the readers to abandon their peacetime understanding of civic and moral virtue, which ultimately entails a willingness to kill (or be killed) even if it seems wrong. The promise of infamy prepares adherents for a meaningful death—both ethical and efficacious. For example, the Christchurch killer explained that victory is impossible without death and sacrifice, noting: "The ideal of a heroic war, without loss, without failure, without some great setback, is idealistic and downright impossible. Even at Vienna in 1683 we Europeans still lost over fourteen thousand good men. That was during a triumphant VICTORY. Do you believe you are better than these men? More deserving of life? More skilled and courageous? You are not. If they could die, so can you. Expect death, expect struggle, expect loss that you will never forget. Do not expect to survive, the only thing you should expect is a true war and to die the death of a true soldier. EXPECT A SOLDIERS FIGHT AND A SOLDIERS DEATH."[52] Purporting to offer a dose of hard-nosed realism, this passage invites readers to reconsider cultural narratives of heroism that omit the grim necessity of mass death during war. The Red Pill antihero, of course, knows better when it comes to the necessity of loss. But what is less obvious here is a shift in what constitutes the "good life" that had been promised to white men over the past fifty years. The El Paso shooter notes that his turn to killing reflected the failure of the American Dream and its promises of upward mobility. He explains that "My whole life I have been preparing for a future that currently doesn't exist. The job of my dreams will likely be automated. Hispanics will take control of the local and state government of my beloved Texas, changing policy to better suit their needs."[53] Like the Christchurch killer, he finds honor in a redemptive "soldiers death," concluding that he was "honored to head the fight to reclaim my country from destruction."[54] If it's true, as many killers have argued, that neoliberal consumer lifestyles have made men soft and effeminate, then the promise of a soldier's death furnishes them with renewed purpose beyond the maximization of individual self-interest and upward mobility, concepts with fleeting symbolic efficiency in late capitalism.

For white terrorists, life *is* war; disparities in birth rates guide military strategy; global migration patterns are tactical maneuvers; and diversity statements are psychological warfare. In the frame of war, life is accorded value through the struggle for existence, not of the individual but the race. The Umpqua Community College assailant noted that "Every country in the world should be a battleground. From the heart of Africa to the deepest depths of Asia blood will flow. Fear not the laws of man, when you get to the other side you will be welcomed."[55] As we observe below, the Umpqua Community College killer espoused a number of occult beliefs that align with broader gore epistemologies, but here we note his characterization of the world as a battlefield, specifically that such a lens should disinhibit white men from the strictures of a peaceful civilian existence. He also suggests that killing offers spiritual rewards from a higher power.

War offers a repository of unassailable masculine archetypes and lends itself to historical comparisons.[56] For instance, the Christchurch killer's obscure reference to the Battle of Vienna above is telling, not simply for his appreciation of the unfathomable scale of death required for victory, but because it was a battle in which the Holy Roman Empire allied with other European Christians to defeat the invading Ottoman army.[57] Although most readers likely know little to nothing about this event, it illustrates the framework in which the author operated. That is, he presents the view that present-day immigration and fertility patterns are fundamentally the same as a military siege on white European homelands. If this is indeed the case, then killing innocent civilians while they shop or visit their houses of worship is a completely justifiable act of self-defense. In the frame of war, acts of daily sustenance and religious practice nourish the "enemy." Of all its functions, the frame of war is a recruitment tool that bribes comfortable and complacent men to exchange their self-defeating and Blue Pill consumer lifestyle for military fatigues and the reward of a "soldier's death."

NECROEMPOWERMENT

Mass killers represent death and sacrifice as intrinsically and spiritually valuable. For example, consider how the Christchurch and Buffalo killers both signed off their manifestos by expressing their hope that they would see their comrades in Valhalla, a reference to the "hall of the slain" from Norse mythology, which refers to a great hall in the afterlife reserved for Vikings who had died honorably in combat.[58] Indeed, Odinism and Norse neopaganism have appeared in the twentieth-century writings of white supremacists, such as David Lane, but have recently been revived within far-right digital ecologies.[59] While white supremacists have appropriated Norse mythology to invest whiteness with metaphysical grandeur,[60] another purpose is to prepare whiteness's foot soldiers for a glorious death in battle. Racist interpretations of Northern European cosmology furnish white supremacists with a spiritual and civilizational inheritance worthy of violent self-defense and self-sacrifice, if necessary. Hence, white terrorists find their own deaths to be ecstatic, meaning that their noble actions on the "battlefield" would extend their life beyond death.[61] Thus, it is not that these killers were indifferent to life as much as they are deeply invested in harnessing death as a form of empowerment. Scholars who study suicide bombing similarly note that the glorification of death and suicide by terrorists is often misunderstood as either a manifestation of mental anguish or of psychotic disassociation, when, in fact, self-destruction or self-immolation reflects an ideological investment in extremist politics, in which death is imagined as "a means to communicate these ideals to the wider community and to inflict physical and symbolic pain and loss on the opponent."[62]

Indeed, there is also a sense that inflicting death on the Other can be understood as an act of racial affinity that bestows honor and power upon the killer. In the words of the Poway Synagogue shooter, "To those who are brave—know that your sacrifice is the greatest act of love for your race."[63] Recent studies on terrorist groups, such as the Islamic State (ISIS), have also illustrated how the glorification of death—as seen, for example, in gruesome beheading videos circulated within digital ecosystems—promises power and narrative purpose to members and potential recruits.[64] Thus, it is not that the assailants render life meaningless per se; instead, they imbue life and death with an *excess* of meaning, a surplus of value that motivates killers to make the jump from word to deed. As the Christchurch killer concludes in his call for others to murder London Mayor Sadiq Khan, "What better sign of the white rebirth than the removal of this invader?"[65] In other words, mass killers *invest* death with value: killing represents a regenerative, cathartic, and recuperative power that imbues whiteness, and killing in the name of whiteness, with spiritual significance.[66]

In one way or another, each manifesto asserts a theory of empowerment grounded in the conjuring of spiritual forces; however, most texts do not reference Christian doctrine to justify killing. Although the Buffalo shooter cherry-picks passages from the Talmud to support his anti-Semitic conspiracy theories, he admits that he has no particular investment in Christianity beyond its association with white nationalism. By contrast, the Poway shooter diverges from other killers in his use of selected Biblical passages to legitimize killing Jews and people of color. In fact, he proselytizes to the reader, claiming that "Christ alone is the only source of life. Know that you are saved in Christ and nothing—not death, nor torture, nor sin—can steal your soul away from God."[67] Although the Poway Synagogue killer's manifesto is explicitly influenced by extreme fundamentalist Christianity, this short passage illustrates a broader pattern in which mass shooters characterize death and sacrifice as transcendent and ecstatic. In the following sentence, the Poway Synagogue assailant's manifesto gives killing a divine mandate: "To the Jew. Your crimes—innumerable. Your deeds—unacceptable. Your lies—everywhere. The European man will rise up and strike your squalid and parasitic race into the dust. And this time there will be nowhere for you to run."[68] According to his logic, his murders are holy insofar as they smite the enemies of God. Such logic traces its way back to previous centuries of anti-Semitic conspiracy theories, such as *The Protocols of the Elders of Zion*, a racist hoax continually resurrected by white Christian nationalists.[69] The assailant connects spiritual salvation to acts of racist violence, sanctifying "the European man" who "rise[s] up and strike[s]" racial others. Presumably, the rewards of such actions are not contained in the secular realm, reaping honor and salvation in the Christian afterlife.[70]

Conversely, the Umpqua Community College manifesto connects empowerment with malevolent and occult forces. Claiming inspiration from Satan, the assailant asserts that his commitment to mass murder empowers him to overcome and avenge his social marginalization. With no job, no girlfriend, and no prospect for the future, he had "been forced to align [him] with demonic forces."[71] He claimed that "I now serve the demonic Heirarchy [*sic*]. When I die will become one of them. A demon. And I will return to kill again and again. I will possess another and you will know my work by my sign, the pentagram will fly again."[72] He argues that his killing and self-sacrifice are meaningful because they purchase him power in the afterlife. As he concludes "My success in Hell is assured."[73] Although contemporary "Satan panics" might prime some readers to blame his killings on the decline in adherence to Christian values, this text is better interpreted as a fantasy of control over the confounding life circumstances of white men who fail to achieve the upward mobility they were promised within neoliberal capitalism. It is impossible to know if the assailant's belief in Satanism and the occult was genuine, but it is ultimately beside the point. The more fundamental issue is that the author locates agency in death and murder, and that those white men who feel aggrieved and marginalized believe they can recover their lost entitlements through violence and suicide. The killer's attraction to occult rhetoric evinces a larger rhetorical investment in death as a symbol of power and control, as a cathected object invested with excessive meaning such that an aggrieved subject might align himself with it to achieve a sense of mastery in the face of radical contingency.[74] The demonic functions metonymically as a sign of absolute power over life and death.

Whether it is in the afterlife or in a triumphant future, most perpetrators assert the belief that they would ultimately be rewarded for their violent deeds. In this regard, white terrorists posit imagined scenarios in which killing and sacrifice purchase them status, reverence, and redemption. For instance, the Christchurch assailant claims, "I do not just expect to be released, but I also expect an eventual Nobel Peace prize. As was awarded to the Terrorist Nelson Mandela once his own people achieved victory and took power. I expect to be freed in 27 years from my incarceration, the same number of years as Mandela, for the same crime."[75] The Poway Synagogue shooter also suggests that, should he live, "when this revolution starts gaining traction (if I am not killed) I expect to be freed from prison and continue the fight."[76] The Buffalo killer also claims, "If we do rise up against the replacers, I expect that I will be let out and honored amongst my people."[77] Although each disavows fame and recognition, they interpret their own violence as a type of accomplishment or accolade that entitles them to the spoils of victory. They construct themselves as revolutionary freedom fighters who will eventually be honored for their valiant sacrifice. To equate genocidal violence with decolonial revolution against apartheid exonerates white supremacists of wrongdoing by celebrating violence in its name as defensive and innocent. Within the frame of war, these men treat killing as an esteemed form of politics, a form of propaganda by the deed, that protects and honors white civilization. They treat themselves as civil rights heroes, or martyrs who fight and sacrifice for the survival of their people. As the Poway Synagogue shooter remarks, "I'd rather die in glory or spend the rest of my life in prison than waste away knowing that I did nothing to stop this evil. It is not in my blood to be a coward."[78] The Christchurch shooter even believs that one day, the history books would ink society's reverence for their horrendous crimes: "An act, which morals you doubt in the present, will be written by your people in wonder and admiration in the books of history."[79] These are delusions, no doubt; however, these passages illustrate white terrorists' investment in strategies of necroempowerment, whereby killing comes to serve as a pathway for ordinary men to achieve historical notoriety and personal redemption. By their own estimation, they are no ordinary soldiers: they are martyrs and saints.

GRIEVABLE LIVES

The glorification of murder and sacrifice cannot conceal the human toll of their destructiveness. Behind the gloss of self-aggrandizement is a trail of unspeakable human misery—of bullets tearing through flesh, lives tragically cut short, families destroyed, communities traumatized. We pause here, near the conclusion to this chapter, to make space for those maimed, dehumanized, and snuffed out—not just by the killer's bullets but by their words that *pornotroped* human bodies into flesh. Underneath rhetoric that aestheticizes, celebrates, and derealizes killing, are people who simply yearned for the same opportunities afforded these men to find a better life for themselves and their families. Their rhetoric obscures the horrific nature of killing, distancing readers from the viscera of flesh, blood, and bone with fantasies of glory, martyrdom, and mastery. These manifestos are not grand political treatises on revolutionary violence; they are, instead, infantile tomes of petty grievances dressed up in a metaphysical worship of death and destruction.

Through tropes of antiheroism and necroempowerment, these assailants contort killing and self-sacrifice into "ethical" acts of communal self-defense, expressions of racial love, and routes to empowerment for precarious white communities, besieged by "invaders," "vermin," "parasites," and "scum."[80] Insofar as the Other's life registers as life at all, the authors' calls for limitless and preemptive self-defense dignify the act of killing, suicide included, and derealize the individuals and groups targeted for extermination.[81] Adopting the frame of war, these assailants interpret the Other's mere existence as a mortal threat to white people. In doing so, these killers mimic forms of state sovereignty that are underwritten by the imperative to maim or kill in the name of life.[82] As Judith Butler argues, "Defense without limit then embodies the principles of attack without limit," or violence without the burden of shame or regard for legal prohibitions against killing.[83] According to the assailants, the demographic crisis of whiteness requires whites to set aside their moral compunctions against murder and reframe violence in the name of white life as defensive and, therefore, justified. As demonstrated in the previous chapter, the killers' antipodal pairing of the innocent white child with the high-fertility immigrant creates two mutually exclusive categories of *grievability*: the former is a grievable subject, briming with life and futurity, the latter an *ungrievable* and monstrous perversion of life. The latter's death is ungrievable not only because it threatens white life but because it also cannot be mapped onto white supremacy's interpretive schema of life and humanness.[84] For these assailants, the act of killing is not murder if the Other is not, definitionally speaking, alive.

3

Ecofascism and the Digital Jeremiad

ALTHOUGH THE PREVIOUS chapters have illustrated how much of the rhetoric of replacement can be traced to the eugenics movement of the twentieth century, several white supremacist terrorists in recent years have espoused a more contemporary addition to right-wing ideology: ecofascism. An offshoot of the environmental movement, ecofascists argue that whites are the only race rational and responsible enough to lessen environmental degradation and solve the climate crisis.[1] Citing a variety of stereotypes, misinformation, and decontextualized data, ecofascists argue that nonwhite countries are chiefly responsible for mass environmental destruction—in large part because of their incessant and irresponsible reproduction.[2] The so-called "population crisis," or the idea that there are not enough resources to meet the needs of humanity's growing numbers, reframes the racist threat imagined by replacement theory in the context of the climate crisis. For ecofascists, nonwhite birth rates are not only the cause of white genocide, they are also the harbingers of an ecological apocalypse. The ecofascist solution to this imagined problem is to institute a global system of environmentally conscious, white nationalist authoritarianism to lessen nonwhite populations through pogroms and genocide.

In this chapter, we analyze the manifestos of three avowed ecofascists: the killers at Christchurch, El Paso, and Buffalo. Each of these assailants staged deadly attacks on unarmed, innocent people of color, living their lives in public spaces and places of worship. Their respective manifestos, released online around the time of each of their attacks, detail the rationale behind these seemingly senseless acts of violence by contextualizing them within the narrative form of what we refer to as the *digital jeremiad*. Following the form of the traditional jeremiad outlined by rhetorical scholar Kurt Ritter, each manifesto identifies a crisis, argues for a specific causal base, and proposes solutions.[3] However, unlike the classic jeremiad, the manifestos do not appeal to traditional US American values. Instead, these digital jeremiads—written by authors from across the globe—appeal to the white nationalist values that underwrite the culture of 4chan/pol/ from which their ideology arose.

While the differences of values between the traditional American jeremiad, rooted in mores and history of the United States, and the digital jeremiad can be seen throughout the manifestos—they all reject democracy, equality, and Christianity—nowhere is the break more evident than in the manifestos' advocacy for "accelerationism."[4] In Marxist theorization, accelerationism is a controversial economic strategy by which leftists purposefully intensify capitalist growth and class distinctions in order to highlight the inherent contradictions of the system. For ecofascists and other far-right ideologues, accelerationism is appropriated as a method of violent social and political destabilization to undermine the liberal status quo through mass panic.

By constructing a quickly escalating crisis in which every child of color represents a direct threat to the white race and the environment, ecofascists imbue a sense of urgency into their manifestos. They argue that action must be taken quickly to disrupt the status quo. Each author contextualizes their public murders as harbingers of chaos that will ultimately ignite a race war and the establishment of an ecofascist world order. Using the form of the digital jeremiad, the manifestos justify each author's acts of violence by contextualizing them within a strategy of accelerationism, wherein all violence has the potential to be revolutionary.

We argue that the digital jeremiad is an important rhetorical innovation with broad implications for contemporary social movements. As globalization and technological advances enable social and political movements to materialize beyond national, cultural, and geographic boundaries, we argue that digital jeremiads may serve as a means to organize loosely affiliated, nonhierarchical internet communities toward collective action. Stripped of the democratic value system that functioned as the a priori feature of the traditional rhetorical form, digital jeremiads are freed from its limitations and embedded imperialism—including the state's monopoly on violence as a legitimate expression of power. The digital jeremiad may serve an important persuasive function for radical movements to strengthen in-group bonds and prompt members toward political engagement outside institutional structures and local cultural norms. Here, we examine ecofascism as an archetypal radical movement that has used the digital jeremiad to mobilize members of its global online community effectively—in this case, toward destructive and reactionary violence against people of color.

ECOFASCISM AND ITS ADHERENTS

Although it has been theorized for decades as a hypothetical political alignment of far-right nationalism and hardline environmentalism, ecofascism has emerged as a serious and sustained ideology only very recently. Sites like 4chan, 8chan, and Reddit, along with messaging apps like Gab and Telegram, which host a variety of radical rightwing ideologies, have created a form of white supremacy "which blames the demise of the environment on overpopulation, immigration, and over-industrialization, problems that followers think could be partly remedied through the mass murder of refugees in Western countries."[5] Unlike the "alt-right," a better known far-right movement that gained notoriety for its memes and ironic disposition during the US presidential election of Donald Trump in 2016, eco-fascists are a self-serious and studious group. Their members analyze and manipulate environmental data, population statistics, Western history, and racist pseudoscience to affirm their belief that people of color are ultimately to blame for the climate crisis. Their memes, when they do appear, lack the ironic plausible deniability of other, irony-clad far-right subcultures. And their manifestos, when they chose to attack, are calls for white people to save the planet by reclaiming their racial dominance.

In 2019, two ecofascists authored manifestos to contextualize their respective acts of terrorism. The Christchurch killer's "The Great Replacement" is arguably the most influential mass shooter ecofascist manifesto. Like others, the text details the myth of replacement but frames the decline of white birth rates within the climate crisis and advocates for environmentalism within nationalist authoritarianism. "The Great Replacement" offers its readers detailed hypothetical scenarios that could result from the accelerationist tactics of white supremacist mass shooters, from turning NATO into a united European army to balkanizing the United States.

Just five months later, the Christchurch shooter's attack inspired an American white nationalist to kill twenty-three people and injured an additional twenty-two at a Walmart in El Paso, Texas. In his manifesto, the El Paso shooter writes, "You call me an ethno-nationalist eco-fascist national socialist if you want, I wouldn't disagree with you."[6] His manifesto, the shortest of the group at just over three pages, is essentially a summary of "The Great Replacement" retooled for the US context. In it, the El Paso shooter argues that Texas is being invaded by immigrants from Mexico at a pace that amounts to a political coup. A large portion of his manifesto blames white US Americans' rabid consumption for the climate crisis and states that the only way to balance their excess is to "decrease the number of people" in the United States.[7]

Finally, we analyze the manifesto connected to the recent attack in Buffalo, New York. In May of 2022, the ecofascist opened fire in a Tops supermarket, murdering ten Black people and injuring three others. The Buffalo shooter livestreamed the attack on the social media platform Twitch, but it was removed by the site in under two minutes. His manifesto, which has been authenticated by police after some early scrutiny, is over 180 pages long. It is heavily inspired by "The Great Replacement," and often defaults to copying the earlier work word for word. However, the Buffalo shooter's manifesto differs from its Christchurch counterpart in several important ways. Whereas "The Great Replacement" describes nonwhite immigrants as an intentional invading force bent on cultural domination and white genocide, the Buffalo shooter positions people of color living in Europe and the United States as mere pawns of larger Jewish conspiracies. In particular, he contends that Black people (the target of his attack) lack the intelligence to intentionally destroy the West; instead, they serve as unknowing agents of chaos who can be manipulated by institutions allegedly controlled by Jewish people. In this section and across his manifesto, the Buffalo shooter relies on dozens of racist memes to bolster his argument, positioning his manifesto as a product of internet subculture we address in the next chapter. He concludes that, while Jewish people should be the ultimate targets of the ecofascist movement, people of color are the more immediate threats and should be eliminated first.

THE DIGITAL JEREMIAD

In this chapter, we argue that the three manifestos composed by the killers at Christchurch, El Paso, and Buffalo take the structure of a jeremiad, or a warning that society has gone astray from some moral or religious ideal and must return to traditions, or it will be destroyed. Adhering to the structure laid out by Ritter, each manifesto 1) identifies a crisis, 2) argues for a specific causal base, and 3) proposes solutions. A storied tool of US American imperialism, the traditional jeremiad is not immune to white supremacy.[8] Yet, the specific appeals that the Christchurch, El Paso, and Buffalo shooters use to further their vision of an authoritarian racial utopia are foreign to the established conventions of the genre, even as they co-opt its form. We argue that these three ecofascist manifestos, which were distributed solely online and were birthed from the ideological cesspool of /pol/, represent a distinct subgroup of the jeremiad genre: the *digital jeremiad*. To understand the ways the digital jeremiad adheres to and differs from its traditional US American counterpart, we briefly trace the history of the genre.

Sacvan Bercovitch originally conceptualized the jeremiad as a distinctly US American rhetorical genre—a Puritan tradition that had been adapted over the centuries to suit the needs of an expanding empire.[9] For the Puritans themselves, the jeremiad served as a warning and a corrective inside the community. As Bercovitch notes, "It is important to distinguish the permeable lines of exclusion drawn by the Puritan jeremiad—its optimistic hope that the people will correct their errors and return to God's favor—from the rigid and impenetrable lines that divided the Puritan self from . . . the heathen."[10] This strict division between the in-group and the out-group is more than just prejudice on the Puritans' part; it is central to the function of the jeremiad. Even as the audience of the jeremiad expanded from members of an insular religious sect to white US Americans more broadly, the notion of US Americans as a homogeneous "chosen people" remained a defining feature of its rhetorical form. As Daniel O. Buehler argues, a rhetor must draw from a common history or self-concept for a jeremiad to persuade an audience effectively to internalize change and "render new ideas culturally meaningful."[11] For early speakers, this meant ignoring all those outside the norm of white Protestantism. However, as US politics evolved and diversified, the genre of the American jeremiad expanded.

The movement to abolish chattel slavery in the United States marked a major shift in the construction and content of the American jeremiad. While previous practitioners of the genre used the jeremiad as a reactionary rhetorical form that reinforced the ideology of dominant groups to justify the US imperial ambitions, Black US Americans exercised the jeremiad's full potential as a means to condemn the hypocrisies of injustice in the United States. Values which white US Americans boastfully laid claim to, e.g., freedom for all, equality under the law, the value of human life, were turned against their masters to highlight the dehumanization and enslavement of thousands of human beings. As Winthrop Jordan notes, the antislavery jeremiad "focused not on the miseries of the victims of slavery but on the wickedness of the victimizers."[12] Rather than ignoring the exclusions that white US Americans had used to structure the nation, the antislavery jeremiad sought to make them visible.[13]

While the anti-slavery jeremiad expanded the utility of the genre beyond its use in reactionary imperialist politics, the structure of the American jeremiad could not escape its reliance on the dominant ideologies of the era. As Buehler notes, this widespread rebirth of the jeremiad effectively tied the rhetoric of liberation in the United States to the very oppressive structures used to justify chattel slavery and other crimes against humanity: white rationality, Protestant moralism, liberal citizenship, and capitalist ownership. Appeals to justice or tyranny were equally dependent on a myth of consensus to which all *true* US Americans subscribed, excluding any form of liberation that white US Americans did not claim for themselves.

The contradictions inherent in justice-oriented jeremiads are readily apparent in the rhetoric of the early environmental movement in the United States. Buehler highlights how Theodore Roosevelt successfully utilized the

American jeremiad to invent a national movement of environmental conservation that remains active to this day. Advocating for the preservation of the American wilderness, the protection of its waterways, and the stewardship of its finite resources, Roosevelt condemned centuries of indiscriminate environmental destruction in the United States. Yet, despite the success of his movement and the good it has engendered, Buehler critiques Roosevelt's conservation jeremiad as an unfortunate reification of the anthropocentric approach to the environment. Rather than admitting that the natural world sustains human existence and thus its preservation is our own, "Roosevelt offered the nation a policy that would bolster its superiority and power over nature—conservation."[14] Preempting the inevitable (and still ubiquitous) objections that conservation is antithetical to colonial enclosure and capitalist privatization, Roosevelt used the jeremiad to frame conservation within the "common sense" of white rationality and the United States' dominance over a "wild" continent.

The history of the American jeremiad has imbued the genre with a complicated and sometimes contradictory legacy. It has been welded to humanize and liberate millions from chattel slavery and abject oppression, but just as often it has entrenched and expanded the imperialist impulses of the nation-state. While the contemporary group of ecofascists who have adapted the genre to their own violent ends are, in some ways, historical outliers, they are not alone in their use of the jeremiad to advance racist and dehumanizing rhetoric. Nor are contemporary ecofascists unique in their use of the jeremiad to commingle environmentalism with white supremacy—Theodore Roosevelt himself pioneered that amalgamation a century ago.[15] But beyond the content and context of its historical uses, the structure of the American jeremiad has important implications for the digital jeremiads contained in ecofascist manifestos. The genre's reliance on prevailing mores and cultural values of the United States—and the presumption of a national consensus about those values—is key to its rhetorical utility *and* its problematic nature.

Ecofascists are far from the first far-right or radical groups to apply the form of the jeremiad. In the United States, the jeremiad has been a major feature of far-right rhetoric for decades.[16] Katherine Henry argues that despite the form's openness to Black innovation, the jeremiad has been thoroughly co-opted by a racist and radical American right.[17] For example, James Sayer and Norbert H. Mills argue that the jeremiad was the organizing right-wing response to the Second Red Scare and enabled the Cold War–era Republican Party to mobilize repressive control over speech and gain national sympathy for their antigovernment ideology.[18] More recently, the US American right has used the jeremiad to affirm white supremacy within an era of global capitalism. Michelle Rodino-Colocino articulates the ways white IT professionals in the United States have framed their increasing economic precarity as the result of an attack by people of color rather than because of the multinational corporations, which are to blame.[19] Despite their obvious incompatibility with US American ideals like freedom and equality, traditional right-wing jeremiads have consistently draped themselves in patriotic rhetoric. For example, white IT professionals draw upon the mythic narrative of the Protestant work ethic to lionize their status as *real* American workers.

While the traditional American jeremiad has demonstrated great flexibility as a tool for far-right repression, it is limited by the boundaries of culture and norms in the United States. For many ecofascists, these boundaries are too limiting for their radical political imaginaries. The movement has a global reach and is not distinctly US American in character (although the majority of its communication is conducted in English). The issues that concern ecofascists are global ones, and their exigency is often unrelated to the domestic politics of the United States. Moreover, ecofascists are unaffiliated with any political institution or party and often actively disassociate from them. Each of the ecofascist terrorists deny being radicalized by traditional political parties or other radical groups. Rather, their ideologies are formed online.

Unlike the US right, the ideological formations and rhetorical appeals of which are distinctly American, the ecofascist community derives its value system from specific internet subcultures rather than a broader public milieu. In the case of ecofascism, its cultural norms and mores have been developed by a loosely affiliated network of YouTube channels, Reddit threads, imageboards like 4chan, memes, and manifestos. The three ecofascist killers take great care to distance themselves from mainstream political parties and radical right-wing organizations alike. In "The Great Replacement," the Christchurch assailant states that he is "not a direct member of any organization or group."[20] The El Paso assailant specifically claims that he was not swayed by Donald Trump, but instead inspired by reading "The Great Replacement" online. We argue that these rhetorical maneuvers serve dual functions. For external or unintended audiences, the killers' claims to be unconnected to other groups lessens the potential political backlash against more mainstream far-right figures, who might be blamed for the violence. For their target audiences, the distancing from mainstream figures bolsters the shooters' credibility, which might be damaged by any association with "normies" or conservatives.

Spurning domestic politics, ecofascist authors agree that their radicalization occurred on the internet. The Christchurch shooter states that he developed his beliefs from "the internet, of course. You will not find the truth anywhere else."[21] Specifically, he cites inspiration from the writings of a white supremacist terrorist who killed nine African Americans in 2015 and a terrorist who was responsible for a deadly attack on the Norwegian government in

2011. The Buffalo shooter is perhaps the most deeply embedded in the culture of /pol/. His manifesto is rife with racist memes circulated on sites like Reddit and 4chan. Like the Christchurch shooter, the Buffalo shooter distances himself from any established political organization. He writes that he developed his beliefs "mostly from the internet. There was little to no influence on my personal beliefs by people I met in person. I read multiple sources of information from all ideologies and decided that my current one is most correct."[22] Directing the appeals to the cultural mores of internet communities that indoctrinated them, the authors are freed from the constraints of the traditional American jeremiad and able to contextualize their own acts of violence within the values of a toxic, racist, and self-aggrandizing internet culture. Ecofascist shooter manifestos each 1) identify and link the crises of environmentalism and the Great Replacement conspiracy, 2) argue that *all* immigrants are enemy combatants whose existence threatens the world, and 3) reframe their senseless violence as the first shots of an invisible global war for control of the West.

CREATING AND CONFLATING CRISES

The first element of the digital jeremiad is to identify a crisis. In the case of ecofascism, the crisis is twofold: the replacement myth of white genocide and the destruction of the environment. Of the former, the Christchurch shooter writes, "It's all about the birth rates."[23] He explains, "To maintain a population the people must achieve a birthrate that reaches replacement fertility levels. In the Western world this is roughly 2.06 births per woman."[24] Birth rates are, of course, are a common economic metric for capitalist societies—laborers are expected to replace their positions on the market from one generation to the next—but ecofascists are not concerned about population as such. By their own admission, the total populations of Western countries are expanding. Ecofascists are concerned that white people, in particular, are not reproducing at a rate that they deem necessary for the continuation of their racial fantasies. The Christchurch shooter warns that "White people are failing to reproduce, failing to create families, failing to have children."[25] He warns white readers, "Every day we become fewer in number, we grow older, we grow weaker. In the end we must return to replacement fertility levels, or it will kill us."[26] The end result, he argues, will be white genocide—the total annihilation of white people and culture from the earth.

This crisis only exists, of course, if one assumes that whiteness is an important genetic characteristic and not a socially constructed category that changes over time based on political, cultural, and historical contexts. Indeed, breaking from traditional appeals to "equality" and shared humanity that characterize modern American jeremiads, the authors of their respective manifestos spend much time explicating pseudo-scientific theories of racial differences and why the white race is unique and superior. In particular, the Buffalo shooter is invested in tracing minute genetic variations within populations and then asserting that these variations are the indisputable basis for widely racist stereotypes he assigns to different groups. His evidence, which mainly comes from widely-circulated memes on the internet, attempts to convince his readers that white people are naturally the most intelligent humans alive and thus must be preserved to ensure the future of humanity—an important argument that previews the next crisis.

The second crisis featured in eco-fascist manifestos is environmental degradation. Each manifesto points to the ways that life on earth is threatened by human activities. As the El Paso shooter writes, "Water sheds around the country, especially in agricultural areas, are being depleted. Fresh water is being polluted from farming and oil drilling operations. Consumer culture is creating thousands of tons of unnecessary plastic waste and electronic waste, and recycling to help slow this down is almost non-existent. Urban sprawl creates inefficient cities which unnecessarily destroys millions of acres of land. We even use god [*sic*] knows how many trees worth of paper towels just to wipe water off our hands."[27]

These vivid examples of environmental degradation show the very real concerns that ecofascists hold, which is an important potential recruitment tool for the moment as the climate continues to worsen. Yet, the actions of these ecofascist killers do not seem to align with their environmental concerns; how does murdering Black people in a supermarket protect watersheds or increase recycling initiatives?

The authors purposefully conflate the environmental crisis with the replacement myth in order to mystify their own ecological inaction. As the Christchurch shooter writes, "Why focus on immigration and birth rates when climate change is such a huge issue? Because they are the same issue, the environment is being destroyed by over population, we Europeans are one of the groups that are not over populating the world. The invaders are the ones over populating the world. Kill the invaders, kill the overpopulation and by doing so save the environment."[28] The Buffalo shooter adds, "There is no Green future with never ending population growth, the ideal green world cannot exist in a world of 100 billion. 50 billion, or even 10 billion people. Continued immigration into Europe is environmental warfare and ultimately destructive to nature itself. The Europe of the future is not one of concrete and steel, smog and wires but a place of forests, lakes, mountains and meadows."[29]

The conflation of environmentalism and white genocide is further cemented by their purported shared cause: immigration. In this passage, foreign immigration is simultaneously blamed for the global growth in population, which Europe continues to lag behind in, and the consumerist lifestyle that predated the immigrants' arrival. Overpopulation simply serves as an ideological justification for racist authoritarianism. The notion that white people are naturally superior stewards of the land is refuted by centuries of destructive environmental practices in Western nations. Yet, the Buffalo killer conflates the protection of the white race with environmental protection, which speaks more directly to ecofascism's investment in the purity of racial stock than in the purity of "forests, lakes, mountains and meadows."

CRAFTING A CAUSE

While the ecofascist movement has delusions of violent grandeur, every ecofascist killer thus far has targeted innocent and unarmed civilians. In order to justify this brutality, each author frames his civilian targets as conniving "invaders," whose innocence is a state of impossibility. As J. David Cisneros illustrates, anti-Latinx immigrant rhetoric conflates southern border crossings with ecological contamination.[30] While Cisneros observes how contamination operates as a violent and dehumanizing metaphor, ecofascists make this figurative trope literal. As the Buffalo shooter argues, "We are experiencing an invasion on a level never seen before in history. Millions of people pouring across our borders, legally."[31] Not only are immigrants framed as an invading army, but they are also made responsible for unimaginable destruction. "Pouring" and "flooding" across borders conflates immigrants with natural or human-induced disasters, and, therefore, public murder is simply the restoration of ecological balance. Similarly, the Christchurch shooter argues that "mass immigration will disenfranchise us, subvert our nations, destroy our communities, destroy our ethnic binds, destroy our cultures, destroy our peoples."[32] Using this framing, the El Paso shooter denies that his attack was unprompted. He argues, "They are the instigators, not me. I am simply defending my country from cultural and ethnic replacement brought on by an invasion."[33] Combined, the shooters work to frame their victims not as metaphorical contaminants but as the literal root cause of massive environmental destruction. Aware that the negative optics of killing unarmed civilians for simply existing in a grocery store, place of worship, or Walmart, the authors justify their actions by framing their victims as dangerous invaders; an invasive species of sorts whose population must be managed or a pollutant that must be remediated for environmental health.

Not only did the three ecofascists killers target innocent and unarmed people of color, but they also went to great lengths to encourage others to do the same. For example, the El Paso shooter writes, "Remember: it is not cowardly to pick low hanging fruit. AKA don't attack heavily guarded areas to fulfill your super soldier COD fantasy. Attack low security targets. Even though you might out gun a security guard or policeman, they likely beat you in armor, training and numbers. Do not throw away your life on an unnecessarily dangerous target. If a target seems too hot, live to fight another day."[34] This advice is also echoed by the Buffalo shooter. The choice of a "fruit picking" metaphor again suggests that public murder is benign environmental managerialism. The fact that the targets are unarmed does not make them innocent, but instead "ripe" for murder.

In his manifesto, the Buffalo shooter justifies murdering Black people in a Buffalo supermarket rather than killing high-ranking members of the Jewish cabal he claims are ultimately responsible for white genocide. He writes, "I would like to address the concept of hard and soft targets here. Hard targets are people with strong political powers, such as president's, [*sic*] prime ministers, judge's, [*sic*] media producers, and military leaders. Soft targets include the everyday man, with low, weak political power. To cleanse an area, both must be removed, one cannot only attack the blacks of Buffalo and expect the zog-bot [i.e., those controlled by a Jewish conspiracy] government to fall as well, just as one cannot attack the zog-bot government and expect the blacks to fall. Both have to be addressed, I am simply attacking one at a time."[35]

The Buffalo shooter's justification notwithstanding, there is also a practical consideration for killing "soft targets" who are unarmed: they cannot defend themselves. For all their boasting, the ecofascist mandate to "prioritize high threat level targets" has thus far been discarded for cowardice.[36] Ultimately, the justification lies in the ecofascist solution. The assailants conceive of killing as environmental bioremediation. Thus, they frame public murder as the removal of overpopulated animals or contaminants from the natural environment.

ACCELERATIONISM AS THE SOLUTION

The final element of the digital jeremiad is to propose a solution, and the authors of the ecofascist manifestos took great care to detail how their own acts of violence were part of a broader solution to end white genocide and environmental destruction. The salience of online culture for ecofascist terrorists, combined with the vast geographic distance between them, points to a value system far removed from the US-centric assumptions of the traditional jeremiad. Rather, ecofascists evoke the values and mores of their online community to frame their rhetorical appeals. American values of equality, civic engagement, and democracy are rejected, often explicitly, for eco-fascist ideals of racial hierarchy, violence, and authoritarian control. While these appeals are not calibrated to the palate of the mainstream American public, they nonetheless have powerful sway over their intended audiences across multiple continents. Freed from the norms of American civility, each manifesto argues that violence is the only valid rhetorical response to white genocide and the climate crisis. Specifically, they articulate that seemingly random acts of violence against people of color in Western countries is a valid tactic, which they term accelerationism.

Across the three manifestos, the respective authors emphasize their intentions to sow chaos and destabilize the political climate as a means to hasten the establishment of environmentally conscious racial authoritarianism. This strategy of intensification, or "accelerationism," is a loose adaptation of the Marxist belief that the contradictions of capitalism, if left unabated, will inevitably implode and bring about revolutionary economic change. Ecofascists, bereft of any serious theory of revolution, view accelerationism as a simple chain reaction of attacks and counterattacks that will eventually escalate into a global race war. While their exact methods of accelerationism differ—they are particular to the shooter's geographic and temporal setting—a three-part strategy emerged: 1) generate distrust between racial groups and destabilize multiculturalism, 2) radicalize white people against democratic solutions to maintain white supremacy, and 3) incite mass racial warfare. Combined, this strategy for accelerationism positions each ecofascist terrorist attack as a harbinger of further violence; the violence enacted by the manifestos' authors are justified as *rhetorical acts* rather than as senseless acts of destruction on innocent civilians.

DIVIDE AND DESTABILIZE

Each of the authors positions his attack as the vanguard of the first wave of accelerationism. As the Christchurch shooter writes, the goal of the current stage of eco-fascist accelerationism is "to create an atmosphere of fear and change in which drastic, powerful and revolutionary action can occur."[37] And because ecofascism is a global movement and these three killings were spread across three continents, the three manifestos differ in their exact plans to destabilize Western multiculturalism. For those facing an influx of Muslim refugees, the goal is to "create an environment where the practice of Islam is made difficult" in Western countries.[38] Rather than isolated attacks on random individuals, ecofascist terrorists argue that their actions are a means to undermine the cohesion of nonwhite assimilation into Western societies. For the Christchurch shooter, the ultimate goal of such accelerationist practices is "to drive a wedge between the nations of NATO that are European and the Turks that also make a part of the NATO forces, thereby turning NATO once more into a united European army and pushing Turkey once more back to the true position of a foreign, enemy force."[39]

In the political context of the United States, all three authors are in agreement: gun rights are the wedge issue mostly likely to destabilize the fragile peace between whites and nonwhites. In the Q&A section of his manifesto, the Buffalo shooter asks, "Won't your attack result in calls for the removal of gun rights in the United States?"[40] His response is telling. He writes, "Yes, that is the plan all along, you said you would fight to protect your rights and the constitution, soon will come the time."[41] The Christchurch shooter predicts his attack may help spur a "conflict between the two ideologies within the United States on the ownership of firearms in order to further the social, cultural, political and racial divide within the United States."[42] Such an ideological conflict could spiral into a second Civil War that would ultimately "balkanize the US along political, cultural and, most importantly, racial lines."[43] The end goal, according to the Christchurch shooter, is not only a practical political one—it is rhetorical. He writes, "THE MYTH OF THE MELTING POT MUST END, AND WITH IT THE MYTH OF THE EGALITARIAN NATION."[44]

This contextualization of each author's respective attacks—as part of a broader wave of destabilization—works to assure the reader (and perhaps the author) that targeting innocent people can be justified. Their cowardly attacks on innocent and unarmed civilians are reframed as acts of bravery in an imaged cultural civil war. As the El Paso shooter contends, "My whole life I have been preparing for a future that currently doesn't exist. The job of my dreams will likely be automated. Hispanics will take control of the local and state government of my beloved Texas, changing policy to better suit their needs. They will turn Texas into an instrument of a political coup which will hasten the destruction of our country. The environment is getting worse by the year."[45] Rather than working to solve the issues they perceive to be insurmountable, the respective mass shooters position their killings as part of a larger confrontation that may accelerate the destruction of modern society, ultimately liberating whites from their perceived oppression.

The ecofascist strategy of accelerationism also justifies random, racist attacks in the stead of real environmental action. As the Christchurch shooter himself questions, "Why focus on immigration and birth rates when climate change is such a huge issue?"[46] His answer, and the answer implicit in each ecofascist attack, is that the killing of innocent people is an indirect means to solving the climate crisis. He continues, "Because they are the same issue, the environment is being destroyed by over population, we Europeans are one of the groups that are not over populating the world. The invaders are the ones over populating the world. Kill the invaders, kill the overpopulation and by doing so save the environment."[47] By effectively conflating nonwhite immigrants with pollutants, these ecofascist authors obfuscate their inaction on environmentalism that may be perceived to contradict their alleged ecological concerns.[48]

RADICALIZE AGAINST DEMOCRACY

The second stage of ecofascist accelerationism, building from previous predictions of the destabilization of Western multiculturalism, is the radicalization of the white masses. To that end, many of the manifestos contain specific appeals to mainstream white audiences. The Oslo shooter claims that his three-part tome "will be of great interest to you whether you are a moderate or a more dedicated cultural conservative/nationalist."[49] Similarly, the Christchurch shooter manifesto has an entire section that addresses white conservatives. To them, he writes, "Ask yourself, truly, what has modern conservatism managed to conserve? What does it seek to conserve? The natural environment? Western Culture? Ethnic autonomy? Religion? The nation? The race?"[50] The implied answer is, "no." More radical action is needed to preserve white supremacy, and ecofascism offers whites an environmentally conscious solution.

Each respective manifesto bemoans the mainstream disregard for the environment and argues that radical action must be taken. The El Paso shooter observed, "The American lifestyle affords our citizens an incredible quality of life. However, our lifestyle is destroying the environment of our country. The decimation of the environment is creating a massive burden for future generations. . . . Water sheds around the country, especially in agricultural areas, are being depleted. Fresh water is being polluted from farming and oil drilling operations. Consumer culture is creating thousands of tons of unnecessary plastic waste and electronic waste, and recycling to help slow this down is almost non-existent. Urban sprawl creates inefficient cities which unnecessarily destroys millions of acres of land."[51]

The Christchurch shooter argues that white disregard for the environment is the result of "the current nihilistic, hedonistic, individualistic insanity that has taken control of Western thought"[52] He continues, "There is no Conservatism without nature, there is no nationalism without environmentalism, the natural environment of our lands shaped us just as we shaped it. We were born from our lands and our own culture was molded by these same lands. The protection and preservation of these lands is of the same importance as the protection and preservation of our own ideals and beliefs."[53] In these passages, the killer conflates the preservation of white racial stock with a land-based ethic, suggesting that environmental protection naturally arises from white racial consciousness. For him, real (environmental) conservativism necessitates abandonment of individualism for the communal values that only biological race can supply.

In the wake of the replacement myth and very real environmental destruction, ecofascists aim to convince white moderates that peaceful or democratic solutions are futile.[54] As the El Paso shooter argues, "America is rotting from the inside out, and peaceful means to stop this seem to be nearly impossible."[55] The Christchurch shooter objects to any democratic means of oppressing non-white populations, writing, "Democracy is mob rule and the mob itself is ruled by our enemies. The global and corporate-run press controls them, the education system (long since fallen to the long march through the institutions carried out by the marxists) controls them, the state (long since heavily lost to its corporate backers) controls them and the anti-white media machine controls them. Do not suffer under the delusion of an effortless, riskless democratic victory."[56]

Rejecting democratic means for maintaining white supremacy and saving the environment, these authors seek to radicalize their audience further. The point is to convince readers that democracy is a fantasy and that only revolutionary violence is a realistic alternative. Marxists are not revolutionaries but rather counterrevolutionaries, committed to maintaining the status quo. The author characterizes the opposition as a "machine" that denaturalizes their political commitment. Ecofascists, by contrast, are aligned with the natural world, and violence carried out it in its name is necessary to eradicate a mechanistic world order. As the Christchurch shooter explains, "The radicalization of young Western men is not just unavoidable, but inevitable. It should come as no shock that European men, in every nation, and on every continent are turning to radical notions and methods to combat the social and moral decay of their nations and the continued ethnic replacement of their people."[57] While most concede that the process of radicalization will be achieved slowly through the destabilization of multicultural societies, ultimately, the goal of this stage of accelerationism is to gain the support of the white masses for an authoritarian solution to maintaining white supremacy. As the Christchurch shooter surmises, "While the movement itself, at least in the vanguard stage, does not need to have the support of the entire population, eventually we will need our people to join our new society, and voluntarily."[58] While white people may be convinced to join the ecofascist movement voluntarily, the end goal is always domination through racial violence.

RACIAL VIOLENCE AND REVOLUTION

Once multicultural societies are thrown into chaos and the white masses are radicalized against democratic solutions, the third and final stage of ecofascist accelerationism is to spark widespread racial violence toward the establishment of a white supremacist authoritarian system. The Christchurch shooter contends that individual ecofascist attacks are meant to "incite violence, retaliation and further divide between the European people and the invaders currently occupying European soil."[59] He envisions a series of escalating attacks and counterattacks; a warzone which "agitate[s] the political enemies of my people into action, to cause them to overextend their own hand and experience the eventual and inevitable backlash as a result."[60] For ecofascists, violence is viewed as the only effective tool for racial dominance and environmental safekeeping. As the Buffalo shooter writes, "There is no nation in the world that wasn't founded by, or maintained by, the use of force. Force is power. History is the history of power. Violence is power and violence is the reality of history. Violence is the only way to make real change in the world. The reason why peaceful protests are allowed is because they don't make an actual difference."[61] For ecofascists, racial and environmental futurities can only be assured via violence, and the goal of ecofascist accelerationism to remove all other options.

The ideal targets for ecofascist ire differ based on which white supremacist conspiracy the gunman blames the Oslo shooter, for example, believes "cultural Marxists" had infiltrated all Western institutions and should be eliminated, whereas the Buffalo shooter blames Jewish conspirators and argues for their death. As a group, they express ambitions of killing high-profile people whose deaths would cause widespread panic and further violence. The Christchurch shooter writes that "there are well known enemies of our nations, enemies of our race that freely walk through our societies, heads held high, believing themselves untouchable. They will soon find out how wrong they truly are. Traitors deserve a traitors death. No matter if it takes 3 years or 30 years, these people must pay for their disgusting attacks upon our race."[62] He goes so far as to profile three: former German chancellor Angela Merkel, Turkish president Recep Tayyip Erdoğan, and Sadiq Khan, the mayor of London. The Buffalo shooter, in line with his antisemitic views, replaces Merkel with Jewish billionaire George Soros. For them, public murder is not a senseless act of violence by a revolutionary pogrom but instead is a signal to other revolutionaries that the time for violence is now.

RACE AND THE CLIMATE CRISIS

Ecofascists manifestos are the products of the internet cultures that inspire and distribute them. In this chapter, we have argued that the manifestos adapt a classic rhetorical form—the jeremiad—for the age of the internet. Freed from the constraints of American ideals of equality, democracy, and civility, digital jeremiads speak to the mores of the internet communities that produce them. In the case of ecofascists, the depths of /pol/ have produced a culture of violence, environmentalism, and white supremacy without borders. Speaking to their intended audiences, the three shooter manifestos articulate a vision of the future in which racial violence is the only solution to the climate crisis. Using the three-part structure of the digital jeremiad, each shooter 1) identifies and links the crises of environmentalism and the Great Replacement conspiracy, 2) argues that *all* immigrants are enemy combatants whose existence threatens the world, and 3) reframes their cowardly actions as the courageous first shots in an escalating—if invisible—global war for control of the West. Co-opting and debasing the Marxist theory of accelerationism, ecofascists seek to generate distrust between racial groups and destabilize multiculturalism, radicalize white people against democratic solutions to maintaining white supremacy, and ultimately seek to incite mass racial warfare. Importantly, these rhetorical moves would be impossible using the traditional American jeremiad and very difficult to accomplish without its form. We argue that the success of the ecofascist movement, which has claimed lives across continents, can be credited to its ability to combine rhetorical innovation with regressive ideals fostered by internet ecosystems.

4

Crtl+V Fascism

On October 12, 2022, a nineteen-year old man murdered two individuals outside of a popular Bratislava, Slovakia, gay bar before dying by suicide. In a sixty-five-page manifesto posted to Twitter and 4chan, the assailant retread the same worn claims espoused in other white terrorist manifestos featured in the previous chapters, including anti-Semitic replacement theories, antiqueer and antitransgender hate, militant accelerationism, and glorifications of mass violence. Like other white nationalists, he repurposed esoteric internet memes, copied and pasted block text from other manifestos, and cited other white terrorists, including the Buffalo, Christchurch, and Poway Synagogue shooters, as inspiration for his attack. Devoid of originality, his screed mirrors the formal structure of other manifestos, including a lengthy justificatory narrative, a question-and-answer or FAQ ("frequently asked questions") section, details about his armaments and tactical plan, and an explicit call to arms. Although it is easy to surmise that much of his rhetoric is plagiarized or otherwise largely derivative, the formal structure and organization of his prose evince the process of radicalization that takes place in far-right media ecosystems, where imitation *is* precisely the point: to reproduce systematically "martyrs" willing and capable of carrying out acts of terrorism.

For instance, one practice common to digital white supremacist ecosystems is the sanctification of mass murderers, including the Christchurch, Buffalo, and the Isle Vista assailants.[1] Eventually canonized online, the Bratislava shooter followed the pathway to so-called "sainthood" through the practice of imitation: 1) commit an act of murder in the name of white supremacy; 2) construct a manifesto containing an explanatory narrative, an ideological justification for violence, tactical lessons from the attack; and 3) issue a call to arms. But sanctification has much less to do with original contributions than it does with the formal repetition of violent patterns of thought and behavior.

Indeed, another clue as to the formal significance of imitation in the fomentation of far-right violence comes from the Bratislava shooter's references to "Terrorgram," a loose network of encrypted channels and accounts on the instant messaging application Telegram, which largely comprises subscribers who promote neofascist principles and aesthetics, accelerationism, white supremacist violence, bomb making, and other forms of terrorism.[2] The assailant thanked the media collective in his manifesto for "some issues, concepts and things that anyone who seeks to fight ZOG [Zionist Occupation Government] should know" and for providing the "practical means" to carry out his attack. Populated with members of neo-Nazi organizations, such as Atomwaffen Division, Feuerkrieg Division, and The Base, Telegram "offers a one-stop shop for extremists," including propaganda videos, zines, artwork, and archives of white terrorist manifestos and chat logs.[3] In other words, digital networks provide archival resources that aid in the process of radicalization and provide resources for imitation. Kyle R. Larson and Guy F. McHendry characterize this material as a "copy-and-paste rhetoric" that enables white nationalists to "swarm" and shout down opponents rapidly online.[4] White nationalism is as much a form as it is ideological content.

Thus, our analysis here diverges from previous chapters by shifting attention from a dissection of argumentative content to theorizing the formal dimensions of manifestos in order to make sense of their seemingly unoriginal and imitative style. That is to say, this clandestine clearinghouse of ostensibly "fair use" material—manifestos, memes, art, and other obscene material quickly removed by most internet service providers—gestures at the significance of *mimêsis* in the reproduction of white nationalist ideology. In this chapter, we argue that the mimicry of previously established forms and practices is a method of propaganda that invites others to sacrifice themselves for the cause.

As Kirt H. Wilson observes, US educational philosophers in the nineteenth and twentieth centuries—inspired by the classical rhetorical canon of *mimêsis*—believed that imitative writing and speaking of grand exemplars trained white pupils in the habits of Republican citizenship.[5] In other words, *mimêsis* was practice for properly conducting oneself in civil society. *Mimêsis* can engender bodily habits that might condition subjects to adhere to the norms of a particular rhetorical culture. Observing the recurrent character of tropes and enthymemes, Michele Kennerly and Damien S. Pfister add that "rhetorical culture is a 'culture of the copy,' or in a more processual sense, a culture of copying."[6] Copying, however, is not mindless repetition devoid of reason; rather, "mimêsis builds on the material action and life but twists and tweaks it in ways that please those who make and those who encounter it, since the former have to exercise reason to make renders and the latter have to exercise reason to recognize what has been rendered?"[7] Despite their disdain for democracy, white nationalists similarly approach *mimêsis* as participation in the rhetorical culture of /pol/, a set of habits that builds capacities in militant white subjects. For those enculturated into white nationalism, *mimêsis* not only signifies membership in far-right collectives, but also extends the practice of *memeing* into the promulgation of real-world racist violence. While press coverage and popular commentary tend to deride the plagiaristic nature of manifestos, such accounts often overlook the importance of imitation as a digital practice designed to promote radicalization.[8] The reception of these formulaic manifestos by those unfamiliar with how digital networks work often fail to account for how mimicry and formal repetition constitute a method of propaganda designed to intensify the ferocity and speed by which white supremacist ideas can replicate. Thus, we conceive of white terrorist manifestos holistically as memes in and of themselves: they are forms designed to be copied, pasted, and adapted by other individuals. The form invites imitation by others with the purpose of reproducing future acts of mass violence.

In this chapter, we specifically attend to the imitative, copy-and-paste dimensions of white terrorist manifestos. Overflowing with cryptic memes generated on far-right image boards (4chan's /pol/ and /k/ in particular), insider references to obscure doctrines and other aspects of internet culture, and long blocks of copied text, white terrorist manifestos are often purposely confounding to outsiders. This is the case because such manifestos are constructed via memetic practices that are peculiar to far-right ecosystems and are designed to entertain and inspire in-groups and alienate out-groups. In internet parlance, the authors do not engage in the act of plagiarism, but instead the practice of *shitposting*, or the act of flooding conversations with copied or derivative content for the purpose of derailing conversations as well as annoying and embarrassing inexperienced users for sport. Shitposting takes a variety of forms, some of which are more relatively benign (such as "rickrolling," or reposting videos and gifs of Rick Astley's song "Never Gonna Give You Up") and others of which are more malignant (such as flooding threads with violent pornography, anime, racist memes, or other obscene content designed to make an ecosystem unusable or inhospitable to outsiders). We examine three forms of shitposting to illustrate the rhetorical significance of formal repetition in the reproduction of white supremacist violence. First, we examine recurring instances of so-called "copypasta," or block text that can be copied and pasted repeatedly across online forums and social networking sites. On sites such as 4chan, copypasta typically involves users copying and pasting recognizable sticky threads, inside jokes, or other blocks of text in response to naïve or irrelevant comments. Second, we examine the use of insider jargon and repurposed vernacular memes that are used to consummate membership in the /pol/

community and recruit others to the cause. Third, we examine the organization of content according to familiar internet forms, including Reddit AMAs ("ask me anything" interviews with celebrities), YouTube product reviews, and /pol/ and /k/ comment threads. In sum, we argue that these methods of shitposting foil unfamiliar readers, while disguising their authors' deadly sincerity in plain sight. In doing so, shitposting turns violence and white supremacy into bemused entertainment and invites others to follow suit.

EAT YOUR COPYPASTA

With some relatively minor rewording, major portions of the Buffalo and Bratislava shooters' manifestos were copied and pasted directly from the Christchurch shooter's manifesto. Although the authors supplement repurposed text with their own personal anecdotes and justificatory narrative, they follow the same organizational pattern and populate their manuscripts with dozens of recycled anti-Semitic memes and racist imagery. Perhaps the most obvious reproduction in the Buffalo manifesto is that of the Christchurch shooter's mantra:

> This is ethnic replacement.
> This is cultural replacement.
> This is racial replacement.
> This is WHITE GENOCIDE.[9]

Similarly, the Bratislava shooter also imitates the Christchurch shooter's opening line in the introduction to his manifesto: "it's the birthrates, it's the birthrates, it's the birthrates."[10] He replaced "birthrates" with "Jews."[11] All three assailants also reproduce David Lane's *14-words*: "We must secure the existence of our people and a future for white children."[12] Despite being cited frequently by other terrorists as an originator, the Christchurch assailant also recycles portions of block text from popular 4chan memes, white supremacist literature, and internet chatlogs. Derided as plagiarism, the practice is nonetheless common both within white terrorist manifestos and the internet culture that produces them. In this section, we are concerned with the propagandistic function of copy-and-paste block text—commonplace mantras and memes otherwise known as "copypasta"—and its place in far-right digital culture.

Copypasta is block text that can be copied and pasted repeatedly across online forums and social networking sites. It is a portmanteau of the "copy" and "paste" function of a keyboard macro, with the added slang "pasta." In the ecosystems of 4chan, 8chan, and Reddit, copypasta serves a variety of functions: to troll inexperienced users, derail long or tired arguments, or signify one's membership in an exclusive digital fraternity. In other spaces, copypasta serves as the source material for digital storytelling, such as "creepypasta," or user-generated paranormal and horror stories adapted from internet folklore. Though copypasta is a product of the digital era, it shares a likeness to other forms of annoying amateur duplication, including pre-internet chain letters, spam, and so-called "xeroxlore," or photocopy lore, which involve the mass reproduction of jokes, cartoons, and hoaxes through photocopiers and fax machines so that they could be circulate widely.[13] Copypasta reflects the type of "stranger relationality" that organizes and binds users into digital ecosystems—text that can be recycled ad nauseam by virtually anyone but is easily recognizable to the most serious and dedicated members of this corner of digital culture.[14] As it appears in manifestos, copypasta speaks to the assailants' credentials and flags them as a bonafide member of an extremist community.

Although copypasta reflects some of the affordances of spreadable media,[15] Robert Topinka argues that its deployment by the far right is antithetical to the logic of virality.[16] The point of copypasta is not to spread ideas but to halt conversations and stunt ideational development. Topinka argues that copypasta is nonrepresentation insofar as it offers no meaningful connections between signifiers; that is, copypasta is form *absent* content. Thus, he observes that copypasta cannot be read for its underlying meaning; in fact, copypasta lays a trap for those who misunderstand block text as meaningful. As such, it operates as a reactionary textual form, designed to halt the flow of words, "foreclosing on the possibility of a new order that might resist the present."[17] Thus, its ideology lies not in representational content alone but instead in its forms—forms that court and coordinate violent affects. He explains that "the humble copypasta offers an archetypical example of this kind of repetitive, performative anti-discourse that discharges affect through contribution rather than content."[18] Copypasta contains no message and circulates only among those already familiar with it. That is to say, copypasta is not read and interpreted, but rather, *recognized*.

To this understanding, we add that copypasta is a ritual of incessant repetition that garners enjoyment for users. The repetition builds adherence even though the text itself is ostensibly meaningless: the form courts and fosters hateful affect, which, in turn, engenders extreme beliefs. This enjoyment matters: the mindless and continual reposting of old text rehearses practices of subjectivity in a digital environment. We might consider copypasta a practice of compulsive repetition that anchors the digital subject in the symbolic at the level of form. As Joshua Gunn writes of form, recuring patterns of speech and the rhetorical situations to which they respond are "the signature of an affective apparatus that both presumes and produces bodies-in-feeling."[19] In this way, copypasta takes the form of propaganda that excites and incites mimicry.

To illustrate this point, copypasta can be understood through a psychoanalytical procedure. Slavoj Žižek notes that in *The Interpretation of Dreams*, Freud argues that dreams present series of "false images," which are ultimately devoid of any symbolic content. Like a detective at a murder scene, the analyst must confront a false image put together by a subject "in order to efface the traces of his act."[20] Consider the way in which a murderer might attempt to stage a crime scene to mislead investigators as to the meaning of appearances. Here, the detective's task is to "denature it by first discovering the inconspicuous details that stick out, that do not fit into the frame of the surface image."[21] Žižek uses Agatha Christie's *The ABC Murders* to illustrate a core principle that governs the relationship between rhetoric, formal patterns, and psychoanalysis; namely, that there is no inherent relationship between signifiers, hence subjects labor and invest in connections even though they are arbitrary.[22] In the series, a string of murders takes place in which it appears that a pathological serial killer is choosing victims based on an alphabetic code. Yet, the murderer is not killing for pathological reasons, but instead is attempting to disguise his self-interested motive in killing one particular individual (so that the murders would be seen as the work of a psychopath).

The trap laid for us is in attempting to decipher the code: the pattern is not meaningful, but the murderer is aware that detectives (and subjects in general) tend to invest meaning into meaningless patterns (much like astrology or coincidence). Žižek writes that "the solution is not arrived at by scrutinizing possible hidden meaning of the surface impression . . . it is precisely by indulging in this kind of deliberation that we fall into a trap. The only proper procedure is to put in parentheses the field of meaning imposed upon us by the deceitful first impression and to devote all our attention to the details abstracted from their inclusion in the imposed field of meaning."[23] If critics are to be smart detectives, like Inspector Poirot, it is vital that we grasp that meaning of the pattern is located solely in the fact that others will think the pattern has meaning. The purpose of copypasta, then, is virtually the same: to lure readers in with the appearance of meaning, only to embarrass naïve investigators for their credulity.[24] Like Christie's assailant, white terrorists divert attention from their sincere investments by creating formal patterns that appear meaningful, yet foil readers into misdiagnosing the killers' motives.

For example, the Christchurch shooter's manifesto deploys copypasta precisely to this effect: to lay a trap for those who would search the text for layers of hidden meaning. One prime example is the author's reproduction of the infamous Navy Seal Copypasta meme, a piece of text that would be very familiar to those steeped in /pol/ culture. Nestled in a series of Q&A responses, the author responds to the hypothetical accusation that "you are a bigot, racist, xenophobe, islamaphobe, nazi, fascist!" with paragraph of threatening text, in which he proclaims to be a Navy Seal, "trained in gorilla [*sic*] warfare" with over "300 confirmed kills" and the ability to "kill you in over seven hundred ways."[25] This out-of-place statement could easily be mistaken for a violent fantasy pulled from videogames or action cinema—an open invitation to moralizing outsiders. However, for insiders, the paragraph is a well-known form of copypasta, routinely deployed to derail conversations performatively and mock inexperienced users. According to *Know Your Meme*, this meme features "a facetious message containing a series of ridiculous claims and grandiose threats that portray the poster as an internet tough guy stereotype."[26] The reference is both an inside joke and an exaggerated caricature of violent masculinity.

The meme's reproduction is also strategic. The meme's placement in the text mocks the incredulous or uninitiated reader and attempts to halt them in their tracks. By drawing overwrought reactions to his grandiose statements, the text would make critics look foolish in their condemnation of satirically violent masculinity, even as an assailant carried out a real-life violent attack. Without knowledge of the reference, critics risk being mocked, disarmed, or silenced in their earnest attempts to examine the underpinnings of white supremacist violence. The meme reproduces not only text, but also the conditions of its habitual usage online, baiting inexperienced readers to react as if the text is meaningful and embarrass themselves for the enjoyment of onlookers. For instance, journalist Robert Evans observes that "the entire manifesto is dotted, liberally, with references to memes and Internet in-jokes that only the extremely online would get. . . . They are meant to distract attention from his more honest points, and to draw the attention of his real intended audience."[27] Thus, before declaring his screed a pathological excess, we offer an alternative framework for scrutinizing meaning as it materializes in surface appearances. We caution critics not to succumb to the booby traps and detours laid to foil unfamiliar readers and disguise the Christchurch assailant's deadly sincerity. The text is a rhetorical funhouse mirror that warps and distorts readers' perceptions, masking its candid racist investments with playful memetic copypasta.

What is perhaps more concerning is that assailants who have followed the Christchurch shooter have transformed his manifesto into copypasta by repurposing both large swaths of text and reproducing its same formal structure. We contend that this practice constitutes a form of propaganda that reproduces its desired effect through constant repetition. Propaganda achieves adherence through the unique interplay of ritual and ad nauseum argumentation, both of which are amplified by the technical capacity for mass (re)production and broadcasting.[28] Consider, for instance, Walter Benjamin's comments about the aestheticization of politics, in which he observes how the proliferation of mechanical forms of reproduction enlist the proletarian class in collectivist projects and mass rituals of belonging, otherwise known as propaganda, but without fundamentally rearranging relations of class exploitation. As a result, "the violation of the masses, whom Fascism, with its *Führer* cult, forces to their knees, has its counterpart in the violation of an apparatus which is pressed into the production of ritual values."[29] Copypasta is an example of ritualistic reproduction updated for a digital age, a form that ensnares vulnerable white youth who explore far-right digital ecologies. Drawing from Benjamin, the digital reproduction of culture and politics creates the conditions for fascism, in which critical consciousness is stamped out through the interplay of pure aestheticism and formal ritual.[30]

Following similar lines as Benjamin, Theodore Adorno observes that the "substance" of far-right politics *is* its form (propaganda).[31] That is to say, far-right rhetoric builds adherence through the repetition of forms, intoning the same message over and over again (similar to spam, consumer scams, or clickbait advertising). Adorno writes that in the US context, "There are a relatively small number of recurring, standardized and completely objectified tricks that are very poor and thin in themselves yet, by being constantly repeated, gain a certain propagandist value for these movements."[32] Here repetition matters, because "propaganda is less concerned with the dissemination of an ideology which . . . is too thin to draw in the masses. So propaganda here is primarily a technique of mass psychology."[33] Indeed, far-right rhetoric shares more in common with the ritualistic and aesthetic dimensions of advertising and public relations than it does with the content-centered structure of deliberative democracy. In the words of Adorno's Frankfurt School colleague Herbert Marcuse, far-right propaganda is a form of *anti-art*, or "mimesis without transformation. Collage, montage, dislocation do not change this fact."[34] No matter how creative and playful far-right digital ecologies seem, they are ultimately prosaic and stultifying, insofar as they build adherence and shape subjects' experiences according to a compulsion to reproduce incessantly and mindlessly their own preferred forms—standardized boilerplate arguments and memetic scaffolding that are riddled with fallacious reasoning, lies, and distortions that become true only by virtue of their ceaseless repetition. Such a practice is, in fact, utterly devoid of creativity, as "it deprives art of the very form in which it can create that other reality within the established one—the cosmos of hope."[35] In sum, Adorno, Benjamin, and Marcuse each illustrate how the massification of economic and cultural reproduction offers political belonging through rituals rather than structural transformation—a prerequisite for fascism to flourish.[36] Applied to far-right digital ecologies, copypasta can be understood as an example of a reactionary form that occludes critical political consciousness while dampening the spirit of imagination.[37]

JUST JOKING: LULZ, MAGIC, AND FLOODS

White terrorist manifestos inspired by /pol/ culture are populated with both copy-and-pasted image templates (so-called "image macros") featuring a picture or artwork overlayed with superimposed texts and often impenetrable references to obscure jokes, folklore, and other aspects of internet culture that are likely unfamiliar to outsiders. Often, satirical insider references are disorienting, because they mingle between earnest lines of racist and anti-Semitic hatred and calls to violence. Seemingly, there is a profound tension between the assailants' commitment to real-world violence and their use of playful humor to downplay the seriousness of their actions. This tension arises from what Phillips and Milner characterize as the kind of nihilistic, playpen attitude espoused by the internet's earliest adopters.[38] Trolling, shitposting, and other forms of playful mayhem reflect the belief that what happens on internet does not ultimately matter—that cruelty, obscenity, and offensive jokes are just a game for users' collective amusement. The concept of lulz emerge as shorthand for this attitude and its affects. Lulz is word that suggests any exchange that takes place in digital space can and should be exploited for amusement. User anonymity makes it possible to prank, mock, or even threaten others without fear of repercussions. In this environment, what constitutes a "true threat" becomes incredibly murky and difficult to discern from mere jokes or fantasies. To make matters worse, those who take threats or taunts seriously only intensify the perpetrator's enjoyment by displaying their naïvete—they are "triggered" and "owned" because they cannot take a joke.[39] These assailants' pursuit of lulz reflects how far-right digital ecologies radicalize users by disassociating fantastical violence from its real-world consequences. It is no coincidence that the Christchurch, Buffalo, and Bratislava killers all livestreamed their attacks, as if they were playing a videogame for an audience of Twitch followers. As the Buffalo shooter admits, "I think that live streaming this attack gives me some motivation in the way that I know that some people will be cheering for me."[40] Such an act displays the very dissociative logics featured in their rhetoric.

The manifestos we have analyzed throughout this book vacillate between stable and ironic meanings. The assailants' intermittent use of irony differs from more traditional literary and cinematic treatments of the trope, in which the juxtaposition of figurative and literal meanings help engender new perspectives in the minds of audiences who notice the author's subtle wink.[41] By contrast, the assailants sow doubt about the difference between literal and figurative meaning and about which portions of their screeds are jokes and what portions are deadly serious. Here, Dana Cloud's concept of the "irony bribe" names how a text invites detached enjoyment through simultaneous earnest ideological investment and ironic reflexivity.[42] Writing about so-called "postmodern irony," Helene Shugart similarly observes that "the multiple, complex, and inconsistent messages postmodern, subversive irony advances can be confusing, thereby prompting an audience to dismiss the artifact as incoherent."[43] The point of introjecting ironic jokes into texts justifying genocide and mass murder is not to create "perspectives by incongruity" but instead to amuse "anons" and prank "normies."[44] Thus, the inside joke is a structural feature of manifestos that frame violence as entertainment, or at the very least, deliberately conflate the two.

This approach to irony is particularly evident in the Christchurch manifesto, in which the author refers to himself as a "part time . . . Kebab Removalist" but also just "a regular White man, from a regular family. Who decided to take a stand to ensure a future for my people."[45] This cryptic phrase "kebab removalism" references a 1993 Serbian anti-Muslim propaganda video that later recirculated on /pol/ and /k/ as a racist joke about ethnic cleansing. A Turkish internet user posted the song as a parody, but it soon became popular with white nationalists because it glorified the removal of Muslims from Christian nations.[46] The video was subsequently transformed into a series of memes that would be well-known to audiences steeped in white nationalist ecologies. Note, however, that the distracting memetic reference is followed by a moment of sincerity, in which the assailant confesses that he is an ordinary white man enraptured by the white genocide myth. The reference to the "remove kebab" meme disavows and detracts attention from the earnest embrace of white supremacy that follows. This passage undermines the stable features of a rhetorical genre that engenders earnestness with a joking wink of dissociative irony. Yet, the plainspoken sincerity that follows the joke articulates an investment in white supremacy. This example illustrates how large portions of this text operate in the same fashion as white supremacists' memes: they elicit shock from outsiders, undermine their sense of reality with joking disavowal, and silence any serious discussion of racist speech and violence. The memetic reference normalizes racism with the positive valence of edgy humor (lulz).

Two other examples illustrate the destabilizing interplay of irony and sincerity that insulates racist tropes from adequate scrutiny. First, in response to the question "Were you taught violence and extremism by video games, music, literature, cinema?" The Christchurch shooter responds: "Yes, Spyro the dragon 3 [*sic*] taught me ethno-nationalism. Fortnite trained me to be a killer and to floss on the corpses of my enemies. No."[47] Although those who study gaming culture note that white supremacists have used the social-networking features available on *Fortnite* to recruit new members, it is hard to imagine that a game in which a cartoon dragon solves puzzles in a quest to collect eggs has anything to do with ethnonationalism or violence.[48] This is precisely the point: this ironic statement baits outsiders to moralize about violence and gaming culture in order to coalesce group solidarity and accelerate us and them divisions. Meanwhile, insiders are invited to enjoy the lulz. As is the case with copypasta, the destabilizing interplay of joking and sincerity baits critics to take the *wrong* passages seriously in their search for meaning. But despite the mocking tone, there is a kernel of honesty in this selection. Gaming communities *do* oftentimes traffic in far-right digital ecologies and, at the very least, forge their identities in opposition to the general public. To the extent that gamers often identify as white and male, their oppositional identity implicitly presupposes that us and them divisions also break along racial and gender lines.[49] Moreover, the Christchurch shooter is correct in his own self-assessment: he is neither extraordinary nor heroic. For those already accustomed to the internet culture of "nothing matters," the author's pursuit of lulz makes his violence enjoyable but ultimately derealized. The joke is a disavowal of both the assailant and the audience's responsibility for violence; an invitation or recruiting tool that makes violent white supremacy seem enjoyable—no different than sharing "funny" memes.

Other killers deploy obscure internet jokes as a form of "meme magic," a term that refers to a series of online-generated, occult-influenced beliefs that memes can move events into existence.[50] Those who ascribe to the theory posit that memes have been responsible for everything from plane crashes and murders to the election of President Trump. Meme magic is the digital equivalent of a chain-letter hoax: it is a piece of viral folklore that promises great fortune to those who continue its circulation and tragic misfortune to those who break the chain.[51] First appearing on 8chan, the concept remains extraordinarily popular on /pol/, a place where many mass shooters have been radicalized. The Poway Synagogue manifesto is a valuable case in point. The manifesto implores its recipients to "spread this letter, make memes, shitpost. FIGHT BACK." Specifically, he commands readers to "meme [the Tree of Life Synagogue shooter] back and keep up the memes of [the Christchurch shooter]."[52] This brief fragment of text is illuminating for its homological resonance with other forms of amateur duplication. First, the assailant frames his manifesto as a kind of chain letter, the effect of which is to inspire and bestow good fortune onto those who might pass the letter on to others or imitate his actions. Second, the manifesto attests to the power of meme magic and shitposting to manifest desired outcomes. Although the author does not explicitly suggest that memes alone can will things into existence, he certainly expresses a quasi-mystical viewpoint in which memes can manifest realities, much in the same way that vision boards can make wishes come true or forwarding a send-a-dime letter can bestow good luck upon an individual.[53] The assailant does not so much express a belief in magic per se as much as he affirms readers' faith that memes can augment social reality. As Kelly argues elsewhere, so-called Red Pill discourse is underwritten by this same quasi-religious conviction that memeing and shitposting quite literally reprogram reality.[54]

As with most internet fads and folklore, a clear distinction between ironic play and sincere conviction is impossible to ascertain. While many users approach meme magic as a kind of inside joke or urban legend, others have been inspired to act out and engage in violence. In this regard, the circulation of memes can, in fact, compel audiences to violence. For instance, in 2014 two girls in Wisconsin stabbed another girl nineteen times as a sacrifice to the paranormal creepypasta character Slender Man.[55] In 2016, a man fired an AR-15 into a Washington, DC, area pizza restaurant after reading an internet hoax suggesting that the Comet Ping Pong pizzeria was the site of a satanic pedophile ring led by Hillary Clinton.[56] Of course, online disinformation campaigns and conspiracy theories about the 2020 election inspired hundreds to occupy the US Capitol and attack Capitol police. But most digital hoaxes that spring from far-right digital ecosystems have the more general effect of destabilizing an audience's capacity for basic reality referencing.[57] For example, far-right influencers peddled the myth that white people's ability to tolerate lactose proved their genetic superiority, posting videos of themselves drinking milk and donning milk emojis on their social media profiles.[58] When the popular press expressed outrage, the same users then mocked critics by pointing out that they had fallen for an internet prank. But even if we take these "pranksters" at their word, the refrain of "just joking" makes it hard to discern the difference between ironic advocacy of white supremacy for lulz versus straightforward advocacy of white supremacy.[59] For avowed white supremacists, however, the difference is negligible: both forms of advocacy normalize and spread their beliefs. Thus, the interplay of pranks, jokes, folklore, and hoaxes within far-right digital ecologies disarms critics while making white supremacy look playful, fun, and even magical, regardless of one's level of genuine commitment, particularly when compared to the staunch earnestness of their progressive critics. As the logic goes: come for the memes; stay for the white supremacy.

Although not all white terrorists share the same level of familiarity with common internet folklore, their manifestos are organized according to the logics of meme magic insofar as they blur the boundaries of playful humor and genuinely attempt to manifest real-world violence through mimetic discourse. In Phillips and Milner's words, meme magic cultivates an "*us* that exists in the magical world of the play frame."[60] At the same time, the playfulness of the killers' references to powerful far-right memes, pranks, and internet lore belie the deadly sincerity of their commitment to violence. For instance, the Poway Synagogue shooter listed among his sources of inspiration Adolf Hitler and the Christchurch and Tree of Life Synagogue shooters, but also Moon Man and Pink Guy.[61] Although the former individuals are known mass murderers, the latter are fictional characters derived from internet folklore. The Moon Man is a character appropriated from a 1980s McDonald's ad called "Mac Tonight," which featured a man with a crescent-shaped moon face wearing sunglasses.[62] The image was repurposed in 2015 in a series of white nationalist memes featuring the smirking character in Nazi garb, toting automatic weapons and espousing calls for racist violence. Pink Guy is a character from an amateur YouTube series entitled Filthy Frank, in which the main character wears a pink leotard, raps, and makes absurd faces easily repurposed as reaction gifs. Although he was not appropriated into an ironic icon of white supremacy, Pink Guy has been transformed into a meme frequently deployed as shitposting on /pol/. Referencing these characters presents an inside joke easily recognized by frequent users on /pol/—whom the author refers to throughout the manuscripts as "true anons"—but also offers a disorienting detour into lulz and meme magic.[63] Indeed, the deadly sincerity of claiming inspiration from Hitler is discounted, in the same passage, by references to absurdist humor that putatively showcase /pol/'s clever approach to irony. Paradoxically, the sentence both affirms and disavows the author's commitment to white supremacy. On the one hand, Moon Man is a particularly pernicious meme that showcases the far right's ability to take hostage any cultural icon, destabilize its meaning, and generate lulz through shocking juxtapositions. On the other hand, Pink Guy conveys /pol/'s disdain for earnest discourse and the user's ability to manufacture lulz out of virtually anything, including vile and despicable acts of violence. These references do, however, point to one very serious conviction: memes are a cognitive weapon that can destabilize an audience's perceptions of reality and eradicate earnest prohibitions against violence.

It might be easy to consider inside jokes as the pathological excess of serial killers. But these references are vital recruitment tools because they are forms of "consummatory rhetoric," or what Randall A. Lake theorizes as a ritualized form of community self-address that affirms and enacts the codes, norms, and cultural touchstones of a given community.[64] In this sense, manifestos are ritual enactments of a community's values and beliefs. The assailants' commitment to obscene humor, even as they carry out deadly violence, shores up the audience's commitment to the theories of mayhem, subversion, and deterritorialization that have come to characterize membership in /pol/. The jokes extend and pass along the community's folklore in hope of strengthening their cause and accruing new members. Consider one final example from the Poway Synagogue shooter. In a call to action, he writes that "To those who are brave—know that your sacrifice is the greatest act of love for your race. Your sacrifice will be remembered. Always. KEEP THE MOMENTUM GOING. IT'S FUCKING HAPPENING. McFuggen ebin. :DDD."[65] Although the standard call to arms is endemic to the form, and therefore easily recognizable, the assailant's cultural references would only be immediately recognizable by the most avid /pol/ users (or digital rhetorics scholars). From the deliberate misspelling of "epic" as "ebin"—a reference to Spurdo Spärde, a poorly drawn imageboard character with captions in all caps used to troll newcomers—to the reference of DDD—a spoof internet challenge "Destroy Dick December," in which participants exponentially increase the number of times they masturbate per day—the line is designed to affirm the discourses and cultural practices of the /pol/ community. The manifesto brings those discursive norms and practices into the mainstream and, therefore, consummate the ideological and quasi-spiritual worldview of those who participate in /pol/. Meme magic and lulz are endemic to the community's folklore and, thus, passing them on through the community's preferred rhetorical forms is not only entertainment, but also an enactment of the community's collective agency to transform social reality.

Finally, we consider the deluge of content produced by these manifestos to mirror the process by which /pol/ users "flood the zone," a metaphor that names how online users can generate copious amounts of content to reshape mass-media stories. On the one hand, Damien S. Pfister notes that "flooding the zone" evinces a creative process of invention whereby bloggers can assert influence in a conglomerated media culture.[66] On the other hand, far-right digital ecologies have appropriated this practice to cast doubt about the truth of particular stories about the far-right by producing an overwhelming amount of conflicting and contradictory content. The purpose of this practice is not to persuade but rather to disorient audiences by sowing distrust of dominant media narratives. As former Trump advisor Steve Bannon put it, "The real opposition is the media. And the way to deal with them is to flood the zone with shit."[67] As this abject metaphor suggests, flooding the zone with shit is a form of digital pollution or toxic waste the stench of which nauseates and confuses outsiders. In one sense, this practice accounts for why the manifestos are deliberately contradictory, confounding, and riddled with booby traps and misinformation. In another sense, it also accounts for the extraordinary length of several manifestos. For instance, the Buffalo assailant's manifesto—an excruciating 180 pages—is overloaded with personal information, dozens of copied /pol/ and /k/ memes, lengthy product reviews of weapons and ammunition, and pages of pointless and repetitive material. The manifesto is congested with disinformation; it is a massive content "dump" left for critics to sift through for answers to their crimes but providing no real answers.

Although manifestos stray far from the purpose of inventively reshaping media narratives, the concept of "flooding," or inundating, audiences with vast quantities of nonsense, static, and e-bile makes these manifestos an ideal form of shitposting. As we can attest, it is easy for readers to become overwhelmed and distracted by the sheer number of /pol/ references, memes, copypasta, editorializing, and extraneous content. Instead of aiming at strategies of hegemonic negotiation, flooding is a vector for "common nonsense," what John Smicker refers to as an "anti-hegemonic politics by American white conservatives defined by a combination of articulated techniques meant to secure white conservative minoritarian rule."[68] That is, such tactics are part of a repertoire of nonsense making that, rather than produce a new common sense, encourages publics to disengage from politics altogether and cede rhetorical ground to those who are comfortable in their own "shit." For instance, the Buffalo assailant's manifesto is teeming with debunked and decontextualized statistics, graphs, charts, hyperlinks, and memes suggesting linkages between Blackness and criminality, disease, violence, and low intelligence. One section devotes twenty-three pages to anti-Semitic memes from /pol/, featuring vile caricatures of Jews and laying out their alleged role in perpetrating white genocide. Here content and form converge: the nauseating message advanced in the visual images and text produces the same effect as the ad nauseum repetition and duplication entailed in flooding the zone on internet forums. Page after page is overcrowded with a disorienting amount of propaganda, creating a polluted and toxic digital environment. The effect is not to persuade but to *exhaust*: to assault the reader with so much content that it becomes nearly impossible to refute every nonsensical claim and fallacious argument. Flooding readers with a high volume of racist content creates an inhospitable environment for deliberation by simply wearing down opponents without the stamina to withstand long-form shitposting. Put another way, flooding is a coercive alternative to debating the "merits" of anti-Semitism, anti-Blackness, and the white genocide myth.

Taken as whole, lulz, meme magic, and flooding the zone are digital practices that work by stultifying opponents and encouraging them to disengage entirely from the fight. Each practice is anti-deliberative in that users decline to advance a supportable claim in favor of simply wearing down an interlocuter's stamina and wherewithal to debate. The goal is to render deliberation hostile, confusing, and ultimately pointless. Truth and reality become subjective and uncertain. These forms convey one overarching message to critics: give up.

THE CELEBRITY INFLUENCER

Douglas Kellner argues that mass shootings and terrorism have transformed into ways for alienated white men to garner the kind of media coverage once reserved for celebrities and powerful elites. He observes how some white men who perceive themselves as emasculated by a steady decline in economic mobility and victimized by feminism, the Black freedom struggle, LGBTQA+ visibility, political correctness, and other progressive social changes turned to guns and paramilitary culture to recuperate their lost entitlements. He explains that the "obsession with guns and weapons culture" and "the spectacle of terror" are efforts to reconstruct white men's political identities.[69] As we illustrated in chapter 2, violence is a pathway for aggrieved white men to achieve celebrity and infamy in a media culture organized around violent antiheroes. This is one of the many reasons we have chosen not to use the assailants' names throughout this book. We believe their rhetoric requires critical scrutiny; however, it does not deserve spectatorship. Violence is attention-seeking behavior for white men who mistakenly believe they are invisible victims of structural oppression. Indeed, serial killers and mass murders have a long history of being treated like celebrities in the film literary genre of "true crime."[70] Given the current tenor of public preoccupation with the likes of Ted Bundy and Jeffrey Dahmer, it is hardly surprising that white terrorists would imagine themselves to be the subjects of simultaneous revulsion, fascination, and adoration as well.[71]

Since Kellner's *Guys and Guns Amok* was published in 2008, white terrorists now seek internet stardom throughout the far-right ecologies they inhabit. "Sainthood" and celebrity status within the /pol/ community has become as important as, if not more important than, achieving popular infamy among normies; however, the norms of internet celebrity diverge from more traditional conceptions of fame. Joshua Gamson observes a major transformation in celebrity that accompanied the rise of social media: "celebrity culture is increasingly populated by unexceptional people who have become famous and by stars who have been made ordinary."[72] Alice Marwick also notes that internet "microcelebrity" is organized around the new affordances of digital media, including mediation, visibility, and attention. Microcelebrity is "a mindset and set of techniques in which the subject views his or her friends or followers as an audience or fan base, maintains popularity through ongoing fan management, and carefully constructs and alters his or her online self-presentation to appeal to others."[73] Although mass shooters are incapable of actively cultivating a fan base after their death or imprisonment, they nonetheless organize their manifestos through forms employed by internet influencers and microcelebrities, including Reddit AMAs, FAQs, YouTube product reviews, and selfies. We contend that white terrorist manifestos call for an update to Kellner's argument that is more suited for digitalit: assailants appropriate digital forms that afford influencers and microcelebrities the ability to address their followers and cultivate fandom.[74] Although assailants seek popular infamy, the forms they employ suggest that the more important dynamic of celebrity they pursue is *emulation*, rather than simply adoration or attention.

Although many assailants declared their unimportance as "ordinary" or "average" white guys, they also devote space in their manifestos to their personal biographies, struggles, and tastes. For example, the Buffalo and Umpqua Community College shooters include "about me" and "interest" sections, which detail their personal aggrievements and also their favorite hobbies and interests. The Umpqua Community College assailant's "interests" section feature not only his favorite movies and music, but also his favorite drinks, colors, and food. He invites readers to visit his Kat.cr torrent profile to download his favorite "porno, ebooks, things like that," suggesting that readers might find that they share a lot in common with the him.[75] The Poway Synagogue shooter's FAQ section notes that his favorite song was Chopin's "Scherzo No. 2" and that he is inspired by Ludwig van Beethoven and Jesus Christ.[76] Preceding the FAQ, the Buffalo shooter's "about me" segment featured screen shots of his career aptitude test and supposed selfies of the shooter with his favorite automatic rifles, as well as general details about his life.[77] Even here, this assailant is engaged in shitposting by posting photos not of himself, but instead of alt-right performance artist Sam Hyde, who is associated with a series of 4chan mass-shooting hoaxes.[78]

While earlier killers, such as the Isle Vista and Charleston shooters, did not follow the same organizational pattern, they too documented significant details about their lives as if they would be important for posterity. These examples illustrate that, despite their claims of insignificance, they nonetheless assume that readers will be enamored with their personal histories, motivations, and interests. Each author writes as if his audience might not only identify with them, but alsothat they will find that they share the same interests and experiences that inspired the assailant to kill. This feature highlights not simply that each killer sought fame and notoriety but that they sought to cultivate followers and fans in much the same way as microcelebrities and social media influencers cultivate followers and fans.

This audience dynamic is reinforced through the adoption of FAQs that address what the assailants presume will be common queries and criticism of their actions. These Q&A sections typically focus on issues such as the motivation for their attack and speculation about their political orientation. Though many of the questions are mundane, the form is remarkable because it imagines an audience of followers eager for insights and insider commentary that go beyond common media refrains. For instance, the Umpqua Community College shooter includes questions like "what is your religion?"[79] "how come you've not had a girlfriend?" and "are you mentally ill?" The Poway Synagogue shooter includes questions like "who inspires you?" "How long have you been playing the piano?" and "what is your favorite song to play?"[80] The Buffalo assailant includes questions specifically for "my people/supporters," such as "What are your views?" "Who do you support?" and "Who do you follow?"[81] These simulated questions exemplify the assailants' expectation that their actions might garner fandom, or at the very least the belief that their actions warrant deeper probing into the person behind them. They are questions typically associated with soft news and celebrity puff pieces for popular entertainment magazines and tabloid programs.

But given that the manifestos are the byproduct of digital ecosystems, the Q&A portions mimic the structure of a Reddit AMA ("ask me anything"), a kind of online press conference in which celebrities or persons of notoriety field questions from fans. Though some of the hypothetical queries are directly related to motive, most of the above questions construct an interlocutor who wants to get to know the personality of a beloved or fascinating internet celebrity. It is perhaps no coincidence that the AMA prototype developed on Something Awful's (the precursor to 4chan and other image boards) "Ask/Tell" forums, which focused mostly on average individuals. AMAs are the digital equivalent of the radio call-in show, in which guests of notoriety invite probing questions from fans and listeners. On Reddit, hundreds of people frequently offer themselves up for AMAs about their unique experiences, seeking enough upvotes to be featured in their own thread. In Alexis C. Madrigal's brief history of the Reddit AMA, he notes that the "genius of the AMA" is that it "imports the aspirational norms of honesty and authenticity from pseudonymous Internet forums into a public venue with 2.5 million subscribers."[82] By adopting this form, these killers construct themselves to be public figures or internet celebrities whose fans want to get to know the person behind the persona. Like YouTube and Instagram celebrities, the assailants attempt to build parasocial relations through poses of intimate revelations, vulnerability, and honesty.[83] Their willingness to answer probing personal questions constructs a public persona linked to virtues such as authenticity and "realness"—traits that white men often embrace in contradistinction to the phoniness and effeminacy of mass consumer culture.[84] In this fantasy, the killers conceive of their violence as forging authentic relationships with their "fans."

For many of the shooters, the ideal "fan" is an "anon," or a fellow traveler in the /pol/ community; however, several manifestos also showcase the influence of an adjacent 4chan community /k/, a board devoted to discussions of guns, weapons, and military history, as well as trading in gun-related memes and jokes. Members of this community identify as "kommandos" and distinguish themselves from both older NRA members and the /pol/ community by ostensibly policing discussions of politics on the board. Yet, this dubious distinction is difficult to maintain, given the inherently political nature of guns and the overlap between /k/ and /pol/ users.[85] According to the Centre for Research and Evidence on Security Threats, /k/ provides "detailed instructions on how to use and create weapons" and can be used "as a resource by a potential actor intent on causing harm."[86] Indeed, the El Paso, Bratislava, and Buffalo assailants write extensively about their armaments and tactical preparations using the insider nomenclature and technocratic jargon common to /k/ (as well as Terrorgram).[87] The Buffalo shooter devotes nearly one hundred pages of his manifesto to detailed instructions and evaluations of different types of weapons, such as scopes, silencers, ammunition, magazines, body armor, helmets, packs, headgear, clothing, boots, gloves, and utility belts, for his fellow "gear queers."[88] He pasted several photos of his favorite weapons, including pictures of himself test-firing his weapons in a forest (which, recall, were actually pictures of comedian Sam Hyde from the "Sam Hyde is the Shooter" meme hoax). His involvement in /k/ is also indicated by several oblique terms invented on the board, such as "innawoods" (survivalist slang for escaping to the wilderness in an emergency). In the section titled "gear," the El Paso shooter contrasts the AK-47 and the AR-15 in terms of heat, bullet design, and firing speed. Although he admits being "underprepared," he nonetheless uses enough technical jargon to signify his advanced knowledge of assault rifles.[89] The duplication of /k/ weapon-speak is a not only a gesture to fellow kommandos looking for insights about how to perfect future attacks, but also a case for "sainthood."

Attuned to the dynamics of digital celebrity, weapon-speak also replicates a common form adopted by the internet's top influencers: the product review. In previous chapters, we've discussed the synergy between paramilitary culture and white supremacist movements, noting how the manifestos' preoccupation with weaponry reflects a deadly convergence of survivalism, necroempowerment, and accelerationism that encourages apocalyptic violence. In addition to signaling the influence of /k/ and Terrorgram, the assailants' extensive evaluation of tactical preparations and weaponry mimics the thousands of user-generate product reviews of guns and gear now common to YouTube. Although it looms large, 4chan is only one of many sites and image boards where users are radicalized. Far-right messages pervade popular sites, such as YouTube, where algorithms bring suggested content to users, oftentimes presenting progressively more extreme and polarizing content.[90] For example, users seeking consumer information about guns might start with product reviews for automatic weapons and receive suggested videos about doomsday prepping, accelerationism, or antigovernment conspiracy theories. YouTube is the largest legal and popular repository of user-generated information about guns and paramilitary weaponry, replacing magazines like *Guns & Ammo* and *Soldier of Fortune* as the primary sources of weapons marketing.[91] The top gun influencers on YouTube have generated over a billion views.[92] Aside from /k/ and Terrorgram, YouTube provides vast amounts of free consumer information about automatic weapons, body armor, and paramilitary gear.

In his "reviews," the Buffalo assailant provides hundreds of recommendations for reputable weapon dealers and manufacturers, as well as laboriously detailed information about prices, durability, usability, and efficacy, including promotional codes for discounts and insider tips from professionals. Adopting this genre of internet discourse constructs audiences as followers look to imitate the actions of their favorite influencer. And though product reviews are fairly innocuous when consumed by the average gun hobbyist, they can also be an entry point into the far-right ecosystem. In one sense, evaluating one's armaments and demonstrating expert knowledge of firearms and military tactics builds an ethos with paramilitary enthusiasts on /k/ and beyond. In another sense, the product review also gives fans tips they might implement themselves if they choose to emulate the assailants, much in the same way that a make-up tutorial or cooking instruction video is designed to be replicated by followers honing their skills at home. Moreover, the authors' casual and dispassionate use of "technostrategic" jargon and euphemism might anesthetize readers and distance them from the fact that these armaments will be used to murder unarmed civilians.[93] Ultimately, in imitating the style of /k/ and Terrorgram weapons discourse, white terrorists cultivate an audience dynamic that mimics similar interactions between fans and influencers.

VIOLENCE GONE VIRAL

Scholars who study the circulation of "affect" have observed how different formal structures court different kinds of felt intensities.[94] For example, film scholar Linda Williams's concept of "body genres" elaborates on how different forms of discourse and representation address the body of the spectator, often maligned for inviting involuntary mimicry in the form of tears (melodrama), fears (horror), and even arousal (pornography).[95] Similarly, this chapter is concerned with how different digital forms invite other users to repeat propaganda mindlessly and imitate violent behavior. The forms examined herein train the body to act within the affordance of mimetic discourse; that is, for the user to reproduce, duplicate, recycle, and mimic.

Though such forms bribe users with promises of detached amusement, the affective enjoyment garnered by shitposting is ultimately short-lived; it requiresincreasingly transgressive violations of prohibitions to achieve the same feelings. Hence, reactionary forms of amateur duplication anesthetize users to increasingly violent and racist content, propelling some to enact memetic violence outside of digital ecosystems. Although racist propaganda is disturbingly effective, we hesitate to declare it creative or irreverent. Instead, the copy-and-paste, plug-and-play templates that organize far-right digital rhetoric work to extinguish the creativity of invention and homogenize both thought and action. The purpose of propaganda is not to persuade critics and outsiders but instead to stultify, exhaust, and make us into fools. The purpose is not to invite debate and deliberation but to normalize racist mythology and violence through ad nauseum repetition. The white terrorist manifesto is itself a meme designed with ultimately one purpose in mind: to make racist violence itself go viral.

Epilogue

Allen, Texas, Anytown USA

As we completed a draft of this manuscript, on a placid May afternoon, a man parked his car in front of the Allen Premium Outlets Mall in suburban Dallas, Texas. Dressed in paramilitary gear, the man exited the vehicle brandishing an AR-15 style assault rifle and immediately began firing into a crowd of unsuspecting mall patrons and employees. The alleged suspect killed eight, including children, and injured seven before he was killed by police. Eyewitnesses recounted the sheer terror that seized people in the crowd as they scrambled for their lives, fleeing the scene, or huddling in storage closets and employee passageways until the shooting ceased. One child survived by hiding under his deceased mother, before being rescued. The victims' unspeakable injuries were the kind once only experienced on the battlefield during wartime. An AR-15 small-caliber bullet is so lightweight that it can travel at three times the speed of sound. When the bullet hits a dense target at high velocity, such as a human body, the bullet tumbles and sends shockwaves throughout the body that are so intense that it can shred internal organs or explode a skull.[1] Like the fully automatic military issue M-16, the AR-15 and similar semiautomatic weapons are designed to maim its target—and can be modified to increase the rate of fire—producing injuries so gruesome that journalists often refrain from using detailed descriptions in their reports. Many emergency room doctors report that treating casualties of these types of weapons is their worst nightmare.[2] Though some survive, often little can be done to save the victim of an attack. In addition to being a staggering physical tool, the AR-15 also maims our collective psyches in its capacity to transform any peaceful public, commercial, or religious gathering into a site of mass carnage and death. By the time you read this, it is more than likely that this ritual of gore will have repeated itself.

Like other mass killers, the Allen Mall shooter learned to glorify gore and death within the digital ecology of the far right. Journalistic and law enforcement examinations of the shooter's social media accounts show that the killer posted about and frequented sites that promoted mass shootings, accelerationism, Nazism, and white supremacy. According to an FBI bulletin, "review and triage of the subject's social media accounts revealed hundreds of postings and images to include writings with racially or ethnically motivated violent extremist rhetoric, including neo-Nazi materials and material espousing the supremacy of the white race."[3] His body was inked with multiple white supremacist tattoos, including a Nazi swastika and SS lightning bolts. The traces of this digital influence are reflected by a small patch the killer wore that read "RWDS," which stands for Right Wing Death Squad. The term originated from fascist governments in Central and South America during the 1970s and 1980s, particularly under the Chilean dictatorship of Augusto Pinochet, as a name for the paramilitary units dedicated to killing leftist political opponents. The term was later resurrected by digital white supremacist communities in order to glorify racist political violence, appearing in memes and other discourses that "ironically" defended and praised Pinochet's ruthless reign. One popular t-shirt that appeared at both the Unite the Right rally and the January 6 insurrection read "Pinochet Did Nothing Wrong." The neofascist group the Proud Boys is largely responsible for introducing RWDS and other language glorifying political violence into the far-right vernacular.[4]

Despite overwhelming evidence that the shooter was motivated by white supremacy, the quasi-ironic character of digital ecologies has enabled the far right to disavow his violent deeds. For instance, far-right YouTube celebrity Steven Crowder argued that the RWDS patch did not necessarily indicate that the shooter held right-wing beliefs. Instead, Crowder suggested that the shooter may have been only "trolling," meaning that he wore the inflammatory patch to manipulate and provoke leftist outrage rather than to express a sincere investment in white supremacy and targeted political violence. As we have argued throughout this book, white terrorists often use trolling and shitposting as propaganda techniques to disguise their sincere investments in white supremacy and political violence behind layers of irony for their own amusement. Crowder's suggestion may attempt to sow doubt about the shooter's ideological motivations, but, in actuality, his comments demonstrate our thesis that white terrorists employ memetic discourse and inside jokes to transform violence into entertainment. Whereas far-right digital ecologies have already obliterated the distinction between ironic and sincere white supremacy, killing for the lulz still ultimately normalizes racism and derealizes mass violence. Like Pascal's kneeling parishioner, do such men kill because they believe, or do they believe because they kill? The point is that we will never know the difference.

While elected GOP officials, such as Texas Governor Greg Abbott, rehearsed well-worn pro-gun platitudes blaming the nation's mental health crisis in the wake of the Dallas shooting, far-right influencers "flooded the zone" with baseless conspiracy theories, asserting that the shooting was a hoax, a military psychological operation (PSYOP), or a distraction from the supposedly left-wing motivations of the Nashville Covenant School shooter.[5] Some suggested that Aric Toler, the investigative journalist who verified the shooter's social media accounts, was a deep state operative with an ideological investment in fabricating the subject's ties to the far right. Much like Alex Jones's defamatory statements against the victims of the 2011 Sandy Hook shooting, some (including Twitter CEO Elon Musk) intoned the common far-right mantra that mass shootings are "false flag" operations staged by left-wing "crisis actors" as cover for mass gun confiscation.[6] As dubious as these claims seem, the flood of misinformation created doubt concerning the journalistic and law-enforcement accounts of the shooting in order to divert public attention from how far-right digital ecologies radicalize mass shooters. Polluting digital spaces with disinformation sows sufficient doubt about expert testimony and official sources that it becomes difficult for publics to know whom to trust. Yet, the motivation for these killings is remarkably clear. Thus, reminiscent of the famous quip from the Marx Brothers' film *Duck Soup* (1933), far-right influencers ask us "who are you going to trust—me or your lying eyes?"

Although it is difficult to predict when and where acts of mass violence will occur, the data on mass shootings suggests that their probability is substantially heightened by the proliferation of far-right hate speech, particularly the rhetoric of racial replacement. Mass killings may be unpredictable, but the likely choice of victim is not. In fact, white supremacists commit a vast majority of domestic extremist-related mass murders, targeting immigrants and people of color. According to the Anti-Defamation League and the Center on Extremism, in 2022 alone, twenty-one of the twenty-five extremist murder sprees were linked to white nationalism and far-right extremism.[7] Counterterrorism experts coined the term "stochastic violence" to explain this strong correlation between racist hate speech and acts of mass violence. Although they note that hate speech is not the singular cause of violence, prolonged exposure to dehumanizing discourses that characterize immigrants and other people of color as "replacers," invaders," "vermin," "vipers," "thugs," "rapists," or "bad hombres" from "shithole countries" increases the likelihood that they will be the targets of unpredictable but targeted violence.[8] Stochastic violence mobilizes disgust to trigger intense aversions to racial others, even to such a degree that violence against them does not register as violence at all, but instead comes to be seen as protective or even medicinal. The manifestos we have examined in this book frame white violence as a cure for many contemporary social ills, such as environmental destruction, pandemics, crime, sexual predation, economic inequality, the breakup of the nuclear family, among others.[9] As Lisa Flores observes, racist violence "has a particular agency," meaning that when it is "deemed necessary, whitened violence orders society and ensures its civility."[10] Where "retribution and safety" are concerned, "white masculine aggression is cast not upon victims but upon villains."[11] Although there are many psychological factors that might explain mass killing—many of which are beyond the scope of this book—we can surmise that the ideological factors that explain mass killing include sustained exposure to rhetoric that vilifies racial others as "replacers" and glorifies killing in the name of white futurity. While not everyone who visits /pol/ will be inspired to kill, we have shown that there is a strong correlation between participation in far-right digital ecologies and increasing incidents of racist terror.

The digital influences catalyzing far-right violence may be new, but a longer view evinces how white terrorism has always fulfilled a ritualistic function in white US civic culture. Rituals of violence—compulsively repeated, mimicked, troped, and memed—are performative enactments of white sovereignty over the polity that securitize the borders of white citizenship to contain the threat of race. For instance, Ersula Ore illustrates how the culture of lynching and its legacy of anti-Black police violence is constitutive of white civic culture, a "ritual of citizenship" if you will, that violently excluded Blacks from the constitution of the "the people" and, thus, soothed "white anxiety over the perceived 'blackening' of America."[12] Noting the "civic satisfaction" of anti-immigrant rhetoric, Cristina Beltrán writes that "for those invested in an ideology of whiteness, racial exclusion, violence, and domination *produce* a sense of membership, creating a commonsense understanding of community, opportunity, futurity, and possibility."[13] Racist violence and acts of depravity are not anathema to US democracy; in fact, they partition and militarize borders around the "property of whiteness," creating white community and preserving the exclusive privileges of citizenship for the few.[14] Drawing from scholars such Karma Chávez, Michael Lechuga, and Alexander Wehyilehe, we suggest that white terrorists also employ the medium of flesh, otherwise known as a *pornotrope*, to constitute the "alien" replacer ritualistically—an object whose mere existence is a threat to white futurity and community.[15] While hate speech alchemizes the "replacer" into existence, bullets and shrapnel complete the ritual sacrifice that is required to violently expel the Other in order to preserve and renew the sovereignty of white community.[16]

Of course, most white people likely abhor the violent words and deeds of mass killers. The violent symbolism of /pol/ and other far-right ecosystems would, by design, shock, disgust, and confuse them. The spectacular carnage produced by the assemblage of hate speech and weapons of war represents a traumatic irruption of the real, or that which escapes realization and symbolization.[17] Such ruptures in the fabric of reality must be sutured closed, not simply to domesticate a profound and ineffable sense of dis-ease, but to conceal what these acts of public murder represent. Disavowal and repression—"thoughts and prayers"—are part of the civic ritual of mass violence. That is to say, these patterned responses of condemnation and disgust obscure how mainstream white audiences are structurally implicated in acts of racist violence. As Bryan McCann argues of cultural narratives about serial killers like Ted Bundy, acts of extraordinary depravity engender responses that exceptionalize these figures and their crimes. But for McCann, Bundy's killings represent the return of the "depraved uncanny" of Western modernity, acts that must be disavowed to repress knowledge of the audience's indebtedness to anti-Black violence—in the forms of chattel slavery and genocide—as the precondition for Western sovereignty.[18] He writes that "the narrative of an autonomous masculine agent realizing his desires despite the harm he might do is formally expressive of the individualism and administrative politics of western modernity."[19] McCann argues that disgust masks how acts of extreme depravity are counterparts to the routine police murder of Black people as well as quotidian acts of structural and administrative violence that often escape notice. The difference is in degree rather than kind. Disgust, as a reflexive response to public murder, facilitates an organized "not-knowing," or an "epistemology of ignorance," concerning the long legacy of white supremacist violence and the ways in which it has been employed to contain the upward mobility of people of color.[20]

In analyzing white terrorist manifestos, we hope to have illustrated how racist killers are not originators but rather points of articulation in a continually unfolding history of violence and white supremacist fear of replacement. Memetic violence is both imitative of past violence and a synecdoche for collective fantasies of supremacy, mastery, and conquest. Although data on copycat crimes is sometimes inconclusive, each new incident follows a similar pattern, from the pathway to radicalization down to the same weapon and paramilitary gear used by each assailant.[21] "Organized public violence," as Megan Eatman characterizes it, "follow[s] a script established by previous incidents" and through repetition "contribute[s] to hostile physical and rhetorical environments in which only some subjects can thrive."[22] As Eatman argues, public murder is organized around well-established patterns that prescribe roles to justified (white) perpetrators and not-so-innocent victims of color.[23] Even when the victims seem to be chosen at random, public murder still takes place within the logics of anti-Blackness, wherein white sovereignty is predicated on the production of fungible and pulverized bodies.[24] As Joshua

Gunn puts it, "The gun is a part that stands in for whole fantasies of Western expansionism and self-made men of action."[25] Our emphasis on trope highlights the degree to which far-right digital ecologies hail white men into a historic fraternity of violence and death. These ecologies draw from, remix, and incessantly intone patterned associations between violence and racial supremacy in order to contain demographic shifts that not only threaten white political power, but also cast doubt on the symbolic efficiency of whiteness itself, or the presumed connection between whiteness and humanness.

White genocide rhetoric and replacement conspiracy theories that now flourish in digital environments resurrect a vast array of racial signifiers from the dustbin of anti-Black and anti-Semitic literature, racist population science, eugenics discourse, nativist and anti-immigrant discourse, genocide propaganda, fascist political philosophy, and arcane political doctrines, all of which belabor the arbitrary association between whiteness and supremacy. Public murders offer nothing original; the racist symbolic economy they invoke makes them conduits or vectors for the West's white supremacist inheritance. The point we wish to make here is that these individuals did not have to dig too deeply to find a trove of historically violent doctrines that, once imbibed, poison the conscience, politicize personal failings, and inspire some individuals to make the jump from word to deed. At this historical conjuncture, what is unique is the evolution of far-right digital ecologies that translate older racist doctrines into a memetic form that accelerates the pace of radicalization and spectacularizes racist violence. Although the cognitive effects of digital white supremacy are beyond the scope of this book, we have shown how the ad nauseum repetition of racist tropes in a memetic form invites audiences to *imitate* and *enjoy* participation in ritualistic white supremacist violence.

When we have presented the material from this book in public or discussed it with colleagues, the most common question we have received is "well, then, what do we do?" As rhetorical critics, we often find ourselves to be adept at theorization, contextualization, and interpretation, but less skilled at offering concrete plans of action. Legislation restricting access to assault rifles could certainly mitigate the severity of mass shootings, but, thanks to the lobbying efforts of the National Rifle Association, comprehensive national gun reform in the United States is highly unlikely. Advocates of an unbridled Second Amendment cast even modest gun reform as a precursor to mass gun confiscation and tyranny.[26] Likewise, outright government censorship of hate speech would not withstand First Amendment scrutiny and would likely be counterproductive, given that the far right has appropriated free speech as a rallying cry and recruitment tool.[27] Although social media companies have the legal power to deplatform hateful speech and violent content, users are adept at evading detection, manipulating algorithms, and flooding sites with content.

When companies adopt stricter regulations and deploy artificial intelligence to detect violent content, white supremacists often migrate to more secretive and lawless platforms (such as Gab, Telegram, and BitChute) that tend to be even more extreme.[28] Efforts by companies like Google to scrub the internet of white terrorist manifestos may have inhibited their widespread public consumption; however, these texts circulate with ease throughout the more unregulated platforms as well as the illicit dark web. Supply-side strategies might also include law-enforcement surveillance of social media platforms to detect discursive patterns that might precipitate acts of mass violence, but the evidence suggests that reporting and monitoring has largely failed to predict and induce preventative interventions.[29] Moreover, documented evidence shows that, over the past two decades, white supremacists have infiltrated law-enforcement organizations, potentially compromising antiextremist surveillance.[30] It is important to note that clandestine law-enforcement counterintelligence programs began by monitoring and infiltrating white supremacist organizations such as the Ku Klux Klan and the American Nazi Party in the early twentieth century later became the template for violently suppressing movements for racial and economic justice in the 1960s and 1970s.[31] Thus, we are reluctant to suggest that supply-side measures are adequate to the task of fighting far-right extremism.

If there is an appropriate solution to be found, we believe it is on the demand side. We must ask a difficult question: what makes far-right digital ecologies and the rhetoric of replacement appealing to so many? In the broadest possible sense, the answer to this question demands a rhetorical reframing of white supremacist violence that veers away from characterizations that highlight its exceptional and aberrant qualities toward representations of its more quotidian and normalized dimensions. Especially for white people who openly abhor and resist white supremacist violence, the more complete picture of racial history includes a recognition that white violence has, more often than not, sustained rather than threatened democracy. Although structural factors like declining economic opportunity and the resurgence of racist populism play an important role in the process of radicalization, the data on racist extremism and political violence suggests that the additional influence of far-right digital ecologies acts as an accelerant, much like throwing gasoline on a smoldering fire.[32] We suggest that there need to be both widespread and systemic community intervention programs (including media literacy programs, Holocaust education, and antiracist and antiviolence education) and off ramps for people already embedded in digital white supremacy (like those offered by organizations such as *Life After Hate*).[33] Although censorship is neither legal nor efficacious, there is nothing preventing governments from actively subsidizing deradicalization programs, internet literacy, and counter speech that resists white supremacy. As Herbert Marcuse and Karl Popper both warned in the aftermath of the Nazi regime, the far right will exploit liberal tolerance to promote intolerance and undo the very notion of tolerance itself.[34] The so-called marketplace of ideas will not sort out white supremacy, nor should people of color shoulder the burden of fighting hate speech on their own.[35] At the very least, alienated and isolated white men need to hear other voices that offer hopeful alternatives and resistance to white nationalism when they open their screens looking for answers.

Notes

Introduction

1. The sign was removed in 2017, when the lessee, Brian Bryant, failed to renew the license and pay the fee. See Bill Bowden, "Contentious Signs Jettisoned in North Arkansas City; One Called Diversity 'Code Word for White Genocide,'" *Arkansas Democrat Gazette* (website), Sept. 19, 2017, accessed Feb. 5, 2024.

2. Eduardo Bonilla-Silva, *Racism Without Racists: Color-Blind Racism and the Persistence of Racial Inequality in the United States* (Lanham, MD: Rowman & Littlefield, 2010).

3. James W. Loewen, *Sundown Towns: A Hidden Dimension of American Racism* (New York: New Press, 2018).

4. "A Few Words About Us," Fight White Genocide (website), accessed June 8, 2022.

5. Stephanie L. Hartzell, "Whiteness Feels Good Here: Interrogating White Nationalist Rhetoric on *Stormfront*," *Communication and Critical/Cultural Studies* 17, no. 2 (Mar. 26, 2020): 129–48.

6. Corinne Mitsuye Sugino, "Multicultural Incorporation in Donald Trump's Political Rhetoric," *Southern Communication Journal* 85, no. 3 (May 26, 2020): 191–202.

7. See Ryan Lenz, "Following the White Rabbit," *Intelligence*, Aug. 21, 2013; For more about white supremacist media, see David Neiwert, *Alt-America: The Rise of the Radical Right in the Age of Trump* (New York: Verso, 2017).

8. Barry J. Balleck, *Hate Groups and Extremist Organizations in America: An Encyclopedia* (Santa Barbara, CA: ABC-CLIO, 2019).

9. Jeffrey Kaplan, *Encyclopedia of White Power: A Sourcebook on the Radical Racist Right* (Lanham, MD: Rowman & Littlefield, 2000), 167.

10. *The Turner Diaries* has been linked to two hundred murders and forty terrorist attacks by white nationalists. The perpetrator of the 1995 Oklahoma City Federal Building bombing took direct inspiration from the novel in planning the attack. See J. M. Berger, "The Turner Legacy: The Storied Origins and Enduring Impact of White Nationalism's Deadly Bible," International Centre for

Counter-Terrorism (website), accessed June 6, 2022, *The Hague* 7, no. 8 (Sept. 16, 2016); and Kathleen Belew, *Bring the War Home: The White Power Movement and Paramilitary America* (Cambridge, MA: Harvard University Press, 2019). William Luther Pierce, *The Turner Diaries* (Charlottesville, VA; National Vanguard Books, 1978); Renaud Camus, *The Great Replacement* (Paris, Reinharc, 2011); and Bat Ye'or, *Eurabia: The Euro-Arab Axis* (Frederick, MD: UNKNO books, 2005).

11. Cynthia Miller-Idriss, *Hate in the Homeland: The New Global Far Right* (Princeton, NJ: Princeton University Press, 2022).

12. Alexandra Minna Stern, *Proud Boys and the White Ethnostate: How the Alt-Right Is Warping the American Imagination* (Boston: Beacon Press, 2019).

13. See George Hawley, *Making Sense of the Alt-Right* (New York: Columbia University Press, 2017); and George Hawley, *The Alt-Right: What Everyone Needs to Know®* (New York: Oxford University Press, 2018).

14. Whitney Phillips and Ryan M. Milner, *You Are Here: A Field Guide for Navigating Polarized Speech, Conspiracy Theories, and Our Polluted Media Landscape* (Cambridge, MA: MIT Press, 2021).

15. Heather Suzanne Woods and Leslie A. Hahner, *Make America Meme Again: The Rhetoric of the Alt-Right* (New York: Peter Lang, 2019).

16. Laurie Gries, *Still Life with Rhetoric: A New Materialist Approach for Visual Rhetorics* (Boulder, CO: University Press of Colorado, 2015), 14.

17. Gail Bederman, *Manliness and Civilization: A Cultural History of Gender and Race in the United States, 1880–1917* (Chicago: University of Chicago Press, 2008).

18. Leroy G. Dorsey, *We Are All Americans, Pure and Simple: Theodore Roosevelt and the Myth of Americanism* (Tuscaloosa: University of Alabama Press, 2013).

19. See Jonathan Peter Spiro, *Defending the Master Race: Conservation, Eugenics, and the Legacy of Madison Grant* (Burlington, VT: University of Vermont Press, 2009), 357, 171. Spiro notes that Adolf Hitler claimed to be influenced by Madison Grant's work. In 1923, Ku Klux Klan Grand Wizard Hiram Wesley Evans also praised *The Passing of the Great Race* for confirming his views on miscegenation, anti-immigration, anti-Semitism, and white supremacy.

20. Adam Serwer, "White Nationalism's Deep American Roots," *The Atlantic* (website), Apr. 2019, accessed Feb. 5, 2024.

21. Jared Sexton, *Amalgamation Schemes: Antiblackness and the Critique of Multiracialism* (Minneapolis: University of Minnesota Press, 2008), 23.

22. Ronald W. Greene, *Malthusian Worlds: U.S. Leadership and the Governing of the Population Crisis* (Boulder, CO: Westview Press, 1999), 44.

23. White Power: The Newspaper of White Revolution, no. 24, Feb. 1972 [National Socialist White People's Party publication], *Social Welfare History*

Image Portal (website), Virginia Commonwealth University, accessed Aug. 9, 2022.

24. Matt Koehl, "America: A Racial Mission," *White Power*, 4.

25. See Berel Lang, *Genocide: The Act as Idea* (Philadelphia: University of Pennsylvania Press, 2017); and Norman M. Naimark, *Genocide: A World History* (London: Oxford University Press, 2017).

26. Kenneth Burke, *Attitudes Toward History*, 3rd edition (Berkeley: University of California Press, 1984), 4.

27. Marouf Hasian, "Understanding the Power of Conspiratorial Rhetoric: A Case Study of *The Protocols of the Elders of Zion*," *Communication Studies* 48, no. 3 (Sept. 1997): 195–214.

28. Michael G. Lacy, "White Innocence Heroes: Recovery, Reversals, Paternalism, and David Duke," *Journal of International & Intercultural Communication* 3, no. 3 (Aug. 2010): 206–27.

29. Alexander Laban Hinton, *It Can Happen Here: White Power and the Rising Threat of Genocide in the US* (New York: New York University Press, 2021), 106.

30. David Lane, 88 Precepts, Anti-Defamation League (website), accessed Mar. 5, 2023.

31. Paul Elliott Johnson, *I, the People: The Rhetoric of Conservative Populism in the United States* (Tuscaloosa: University of Alabama Press, 2021).

32. Kathleen Belew, *Bring the War Home: The White Power Movement and Paramilitary America* (Cambridge, MA: Harvard University Press, 2019).

33. Patricia Riley, James F. Klumpp, and Thomas A. Hollihan, "The Dark Side of Community and Democracy: Militias, Patriots and Angry White Guys," in *Argument in a Time of Change: Definitions, Frameworks, and Critiques*, ed. James F. Klumpp (Annandale, VA: National Communication Association, 1997), 202–7.

34. Nancy S. Love, *Trendy Fascism: White Power Music and the Future of Democracy* (Albany: SUNY Press, 2016).

35. Contemporary white nationalists have ditched the skinhead look for a more respectable and polished aesthetic that includes fashionable suits and the signature "undercut" hairstyle. See Eileen G'Sell, "'Dapper' and Dangerous: The Ugly History of Glamorizing White Nationalism," *Salon* (website), Dec. 4, 2016, accessed Feb. 5, 2024.

36. Ian Haney López, *Dog Whistle Politics: How Coded Racial Appeals Have Reinvented Racism and Wrecked the Middle Class* (New York: Oxford University Press, 2015).

37. Vincent Pham, "Our Foreign President Barack Obama: The Racial Logics of Birther Discourses," *Journal of International and Intercultural Communication* 8, no. 2 (2015): 86–107.

38. Bradley A. Serber, "Dog Whistling and Howling: Covert and Overt Hate Speech and Plausible Deniability," in *The Rhetoric of Fascism*, ed. Nathan Crick (Tuscaloosa: University of Alabama Press, 2022).

39. Jason Wilson, "White Nationalist Hate Groups Have Grown 55% in Trump Era, Report Finds," *The Guardian* (website), Mar. 18, 2020, accessed Feb. 5, 2024.

40. Hawley, *Making Sense of the Alt-Right*.

41. Angela Nagle, *Kill All Normies: Online Culture Wars from 4Chan and Tumblr to Trump and the Alt-Right* (London, UK: Zero Books, 2017).

42. See Whitney Phillips and Ryan M. Milner, *The Ambivalent Internet: Mischief, Oddity, and Antagonism Online* (Cambridge, UK: Polity Press, 2017).

43. Alan Finlayson, "Neoliberalism, the Alt-Right and the Intellectual Dark Web," *Theory, Culture & Society* 38, no. 6 (Sept. 6, 2021): 167–90.

44. Carlson and Ingraham quoted in Domenico Montanaro, "How the 'Replacement' Theory Went Mainstream on the Political Right," *NPR* (website), May 17, 2022, accessed Feb. 5, 2024.

45. Matthew Gaetz (@mattgaetz), "@TuckerCarlson is CORRECT about Replacement Theory as he explains what is happening to America. The ADL is a racist organization," Twitter (X), Sept. 25, 2021, 11:52 AM.

46. Theodore Schleifer, "King Doubles Down on Controversial 'Babies' Tweet," *CNN* (website), Mar. 14, 2017, accessed Feb. 5, 2024.

47. King quoted in Schleifer, "King Doubles Down."

48. Montanaro, "How the 'Replacement' Theory."

49. Dylan Rodríguez, *White Reconstruction: Domestic Warfare and the Logics of Genocide* (New York: Fordham University Press, 2020), 3.

50. Paul Elliott Johnson, "Fear of a Black City: Gender and Postracial Sovereignty in *Death Wish* (2018)," *Women's Studies in Communication* 45, no. 2 (July 26, 2021): 232–53.

51. Alexandra Minna Stern, *Proud Boys and the White Ethnostate: How the Alt-Right Is Warping the American Imagination* (Boston, MA: Beacon Press 2019).

52. Eric King Watts, "'Zombies Are Real': Fantasies, Conspiracies, and the Post-Truth Wars," *Philosophy & Rhetoric* 51, no. 4 (2018): 441–70; and Eric King Watts, "Postracial Fantasies, Blackness, and Zombies," *Communication and Critical/Cultural Studies* 14, no. 4 (Oct. 2, 2017): 44.

53. Benedict Anderson, *Imagined Communities: Reflections on the Origin and Spread of Nationalism* (New York: Verso, 1991).

54. Achille Mbembe, *Necropolitics* (Durham, NC: Duke University Press, 2019), 72.

55. J. David Cisneros, "Contaminated Communities: The Metaphor of 'Immigrant as Pollutant' in Media Representations of Immigration," *Rhetoric &*

Public Affairs 11, no. 4 (2008): 569–601; and Lisa A. Flores, *Deportable and Disposable: Public Rhetoric and the Making of the Illegal Immigrant* (University Park: Pennsylvania State University Press, 2020).

56. Judith Butler, *The Force of Nonviolence: An Ethico-Political Bind* (New York: Verso, 2020), 112.

57. Lamiyah Bahrainwala, "Shithole Rhetorics," *Journal of International and Intercultural Communication* 14, no. 3 (Aug. 11, 2020): 185–201.

58. Jeff Tischauser and Kevin Musgrave, "Far-Right Media as Imitated Counterpublicity: A Discourse Analysis on Racial Meaning and Identity on Vdare.Com," *Howard Journal of Communications* 31, no. 3 (Dec. 24, 2019): 282–96.

59. Michael Edison Hayden, "Stephen Miller's Affinity for White Nationalism Revealed in Leaked Emails," Southern Poverty Law Center (website), Nov. 12, 2019, accessed Feb. 6, 2024.

60. Jason Wilson, "White Farmers: How a Far-Right Idea Was Planted in Donald Trump's Mind," *The Guardian* (website), Aug. 24, 2018, accessed Feb. 6, 2024.

61. See Hawley, *Making Sense of the Alt-Right*.

62. Miller-Idriss, *Hate in the Homeland*, 3.

63. See chapter 3 in Phillips and Milner, *You Are Here*.

64. Jenny Edbauer, "Unframing Models of Public Distribution: From Rhetorical Situation to Rhetorical Ecologies," *Rhetoric Society Quarterly* 35, no. 4 (2005): 5–24; Nathaniel A. Rivers and Maarten Derksen, "Ecologies of Deception in Psychology and Rhetoric," *Quarterly Journal of Speech* 101, no. 4 (Nov. 2015): 633–54 ; Nathan Stormer, "Rhetoric's Diverse Materiality: Polythetic Ontology and Genealogy," *Review of Communication* 16, no. 4 (Oct. 2016): 299–316; Nathan Stormer, "Rhetoric by Accident," *Philosophy & Rhetoric* 53, no. 4 (Oct. 2020): 353–76.

65. Edbauer, "Unframing Models of Public Distribution," 9.

66. Phillips and Milner, *You Are Here*.

67. Sy Taffel, *Digital Media Ecologies: Entanglements of Content, Code and Hardware* (New York: Bloomsbury, 2019).

68. Davi Johnson, "Mapping the Meme: A Geographical Approach to Materialist Rhetorical Criticism," *Communication and Critical/Cultural Studies* 4, no. 1 (Mar. 1, 2007): 27–50.

69. Derek M. Sparby, *Memetic Rhetorics: Toward a Toolkit for Ethical Meming* (Ann Arbor: University of Michigan Press, 2023), 17.

70. Sparby, *Memetic Rhetorics*, 17.

71. Woods and Hahner, *Make America Meme Again*, 15.

72. We borrow the metaphor of "stickiness" from Sara Ahmed, who uses the term to connote how individuals become affectively invested in incoherent

far-right ideologies. See Sara Ahmed, *Cultural Politics of Emotion* (Edinburgh: Edinburgh University Press, 2014).

73. For foundational work on rhetorical genres, see Karlyn Kohrs Campbell and Kathleen Hall Jamieson, *Form and Genre: Shaping Rhetorical Action* (Falls Church, VA: Speech Communication Association, 1978); Carolyn R. Miller, "Genre as Social Action," *Quarterly Journal of Speech* 70, no. 2 (May 1, 1984): 151–67; Jackson Harrell and Wil A. Linkugel, "On Rhetorical Genre: An Organizing Perspective," *Philosophy & Rhetoric* 11, no. 4 (1978): 262–81.

74. Caroline Levine, *Forms: Whole, Rhythm, Hierarchy, Network* (Princeton, NJ: Princeton University Press, 2015).

75. Joshua Gunn, "Maranatha," *Quarterly Journal of Speech* 98, no. 4 (Nov. 2012): 364. See also Kenneth Burke, *The Philosophy of Literary Form*, 3rd ed. (Berkeley: University of California Press, 1974).

76. Linda Williams, "Film Bodies: Gender, Genre, and Excess," *Film Quarterly* 44, no. 4 (Summer 1991): 2–13.

77. Janet Lyon, *Manifestoes: Provocations of the Modern* (Ithaca, NY: Cornell University Press, 1999), 3.

78. Karma R. Chavez, *Queer Migration Politics: Activist Rhetoric and Coalitional Possibilities* (Urbana: University of Illinois Press, 2013), 48.

79. José Ángel Maldonado, "Manifestx: Toward a Rhetoric Loaded with Future," *Communication and Critical/Cultural Studies* 17, no. 1 (Mar. 31, 2020): 104.

80. Bryan J. McCann, "Therapeutic and Material <Victim>Hood: Ideology and the Struggle for Meaning in the Illinois Death Penalty Controversy," *Communication and Critical/Cultural Studies* 4, no. 4 (Dec. 1, 2007): 382–401.

81. Richard Branscomb, "Making Manifest: White Supremacist Violence and the Ethics of Alethurgy," *Journal for the History of Rhetoric* 24, no. 2 (May 4, 2021): 143.

82. Richard Pineda, "Inconvenient Horror: Violence as Rhetoric and the El Paso Shooting," *Rhetoric & Public Affairs* 25, no. 3 (2022): 127–43.

83. See also Craig A. Hosterman, "The Rhetoric of Violence," *Communicator* (1978): 9–21; Megan Foley, "Of Violence and Rhetoric: An Ethical Aporia," *Quarterly Journal of Speech* 99, no. 2 (2013): 191–99; Nathan Stormer, "On the Origins of Violence and Language," *Quarterly Journal of Speech* 99, no. 2 (May 2013): 182–90; Jeremy Engels, "The Rhetoric of Violence," *Symplokē* 20, no. 1–2 (2012): 121–38.

84. "Speech plus" is a First Amendment legal doctrine used to protect forms of expression that are symbolic conduct. See Eugene Volokh, "Symbolic Expression and the Original Meaning of the First Amendment," *Georgetown Law Review* 97 (2008): 1057–84.

85. Jay P. Childers, "The Rhetoric of Physical Violence," *Rhetoric and Public Affairs* 25, no. 3 (Sept. 1, 2022): 1–23.

86. Lisa M. Corrigan, "The Gun as (Race/Gender) Technê," in *Rhetoric and Guns*, ed. Lydia Wilkes, Nate Kreuter, and Ryan Skinnell (Logan: Utah State University Press, 2022), 69–82.

87. Wilkes, Kreuter, and Skinnell, "Introduction," in *Rhetoric and Guns*, 8.

88. Bryan J. McCann, "Serial Murder as Modernist Ritual," *Rhetoric and Public Affairs* 25, no. 3 (Sept. 1, 2022): 49–74.

89. E. Chebrolu, "The Racial Lens of Dylann Roof: Racial Anxiety and White Nationalist Rhetoric on New Media," *Review of Communication* 20, no. 1 (Jan. 4, 2020): 47–68.

90. Phobiogenic racism is explored in the work of Frantz Fanon. See Frantz Fanon, *Black Skin, White Masks*, trans. Richard Philcox (New York: Grove Press, 2008).

91. E. Chebrolu, "The Function and Field of Speech and Language in White Nationalist Manifestoes." In *Lacan and Race: Racism, Identity, and Psychoanalytic Theory*, ed. Sheldon George and Derek Hook (New York: Routledge, 2021).

92. Christian Lundberg, *Lacan in Public: Psychoanalysis and the Science of Rhetoric* (Tuscaloosa: University of Alabama Press, 2012).

93. Lundberg, *Lacan in Public*, 5.

94. Kalpana Seshadri-Crooks, *Desiring Whiteness: A Lacanian Analysis of Race* (New York: Routledge, 2000).

95. Stuart Hall, *The Fateful Triangle: Race, Ethnicity, Nation*, ed. Kobena Mercer (Cambridge, MA: Harvard University Press, 2017), 45.

96. Alexander G. Weheliye, *Habeas Viscus: Racializing Assemblages, Biopolitics, and Black Feminist Theories of the Human* (Durham, NC: Duke University Press, 2014).

97. Hortense J. Spillers, "Mama's Baby, Papa's Maybe: An American Grammar Book," *Diacritics* 17, no. 2 (Summer 1987): 65–81; Sylvia Wynter, "Unsettling the Coloniality of Being/Power/Truth/Freedom: Towards the Human, After Man, Its Overrepresentation—An Argument," *CR: The New Centennial Review* 3, no. 3 (2003): 257–337.

98. Saidya V. Hartman, *Scenes of Subjection: Terror, Slavery, and Self-Making in Nineteenth-Century America* (London: Oxford University Press); Calvin L. Warren, *Ontological Terror: Blackness, Nihilism, and Emancipation* (Durham, NC: Duke University Press, 2018).

99. Watts, "Postracial Fantasies."

100. Allison L. Rowland, *Zoetropes and the Politics of Humanhood* (Columbus: Ohio State University Press, 2020).

101. Watts, "'Zombies Are Real,'" 445.

102. See Sigmund Freud, *Beyond the Pleasure Principle* (New York: International Psycho-Analytical Press, 1922); Jacques Lacan, *The Four Fundamental Concepts of Psychoanalysis* (Norton, 1998). See also Joshua Gunn, "Refitting

Fantasy: Psychoanalysis, Subjectivity, and Talking to the Dead," *Quarterly Journal of Speech* 90, no. 1 (Feb. 2004): 1–23; Claire Sisco King and Joshua Gunn, "On a Violence Unseen: The Womanly Object and Sacrificed Man," *Quarterly Journal of Speech* 99, no. 2 (May 1, 2013): 200–208; Lundberg, *Lacan in Public.*

103. Julia Kristeva, *The Power of Horror: An Essay on Abjection* (New York: Columbia University Press, 1982).

104. Slavoj Žižek, "Descartes and the Post-Traumatic Subject: On Catherine Malabou's Les Nouveaux Blessés and Other Autistic Monsters," *Qui Parle* 17, no. 2 (Dec. 1, 2009): 123–47.

105. Todd McGowan, *Enjoying What We Don't Have: The Political Project of Psychoanalysis* (Lincoln: University of Nebraska Press, 2013).

106. Terry Eagleton, *On Evil* (New Haven, CT: Yale University Press, 2011), 77–78.

107. Derek Hook, "What Is 'Enjoyment as a Political Factor?'," *Political Psychology* 38, no. 4 (2017): 614.

108. Joshua Gunn, *Political Perversion: Rhetorical Aberration in the Time of Trumpeteering* (Chicago: University of Chicago Press, 2020).

109. Burke, *The Philosophy of Literary Form*, 191.

Chapter 1

1. William H. Frey, "The US Will Become 'Minority White' in 2045, Census Projects," Brookings (website), Mar. 14, 2018, accessed Feb. 6, 2024.

2. Maureen A. Craig and Jennifer A. Richeson, "More Diverse Yet Less Tolerant? How the Increasingly Diverse Racial Landscape Affects White Americans' Racial Attitudes," *Personality and Social Psychology Bulletin* 40, no. 6 (2014): 750–61.

3. Hinton, *It Can Happen Here.*

4. Denise M. Bostdorff, "Obama, Trump, and Reflections on the Rhetoric of Political Change," *Rhetoric & Public Affairs* 20, no. 4 (2017): 695–706; Joshua Gunn, "On Political Perversion," *Rhetoric Society Quarterly* 48, no. 2 (Mar. 15, 2018): 161–86; Paul Elliott Johnson, "The Art of Masculine Victimhood: Donald Trump's Demagoguery," *Women's Studies in Communication* 40, no. 3 (July 3, 2017): 229–50; Casey R. Kelly, *Apocalypse Man: The Death Drive and the Rhetoric of White Masculine Victimhood* (Columbus: Ohio State University Press, 2020); Casey Ryan Kelly, "Donald J. Trump and the Rhetoric of Ressentiment," *Quarterly Journal of Speech* 106, no. 1 (2020): 2–24; and Robert E. Terrill, "The Post-Racial and Post-Ethical Discourse of Donald J. Trump," *Rhetoric & Public Affairs* 20, no. 3 (2017): 493–510.

5. Linda Martín Alcoff, *The Future of Whiteness* (Cambridge, UK: Polity, 2015), 4.

6. Watts, "Postracial Fantasies," 317–33.

7. Greene, *Malthusian Worlds*, 44.

8. Seshadri-Crooks, *Desiring Whiteness*.

9. Paul E. Johnson names a similar phenomenon of "postracial sovereignty," whereby sovereignty over the body politics is concentrated in white emissaries of the law but without being explicitly named in racial terms. See Johnson, "Fear of a Black City."

10. Mbembe, *Necropolitics*, 72. See also Michel Foucault, *Security, Territory, Population: Lectures at the Collège de France 1977–1978*, ed. Michel Senellart, trans. Graham Burchell (New York: Picador, 2009).

11. Ian Barnard, *Sex Panic Rhetorics, Queer Interventions* (Tuscaloosa: University of Alabama Press, 2020), 7.

12. Stern, *Proud Boys*, 98.

13. Fanon, *Black Skin, White Masks*, 135.

14. Christchurch assailant, "The Great Replacement: Toward a New Society," 15. The authors can provide a copy of the manifesto upon request.

15. Butler, *Nonviolence*, 112.

16. Fanon characterizes "historical-racial schema" as a corporeal grid of intelligibility, organized by the white gaze, that prefigures how racialized subjects perceive their bodily sensations and movements in relation to others. See *Black Skin, White Masks*, 91–92.

17. Tommy J. Curry, *The Man-Not: Race, Class, Genre, and the Dilemmas of Black Manhood* (Philadelphia: Temple University Press, 2017), 91.

18. Hall, *The Fateful Triangle*, 16.

19. Luz Calvo, "Racial Fantasies and the Primal Scene of Miscegenation," *International Journal of Psychoanalysis* 89, no. 1 (Feb. 1, 2008): 55–70.

20. Jean Laplanche and Jean-Bertrand Pontalis, *The Language of Psycho-Analysis*, 6th ed. (New York: Norton, 1973), 349.

21. See Cristina Beltrán, *Cruelty as Citizenship: How Migrant Suffering Sustains White Democracy* (Minneapolis: University of Minnesota Press, 2020); and Flores, *Deportable and Disposable*.

22. McGowan, *Enjoying What We Don't Have*, 120.

23. Chebrolu, "The Racial Lens of Dylann Roof," 3.

24. See Calum Matheson, "'What Does Obama Want of Me?' Anxiety and Jade Helm 15," *Quarterly Journal of Speech* 102, no. 2 (May 2016): 133–49.

25. Curry, *The Man-Not*, 81.

26. McGowan, *Enjoying What We Don't Have*, 50.

27. McGowan, *Enjoying What We Don't Have*, 50.

28. Chetan Bhatt, "White Extinction: Metaphysical Elements of Contemporary Western Fascism," *Theory, Culture & Society* 38, no. 1 (Jan. 1, 2021): 27–52.

29. Bryan J. McCann, "Lonely Young American: Queer Terrorist Recruitment

and the Trope of the Child," *QED: A Journal in GLBTQ Worldmaking* 7, no. 2 (2020): 25–47.

30. Lauren Berlant, *The Queen of America Goes to Washington City: Essays on Sex and Citizenship* (Durham, NC: Duke University Press, 1997).

31. Robin Bernstein, *Racial Innocence: Performing American Childhood from Slavery to Civil Rights* (New York: New York University Press, 2011).

32. See Ersula J. Ore, *Lynching: Violence, Rhetoric, and American Identity* (Jackson: University Press of Mississippi, 2019).

33. Erin J. Rand, "PROTECTing the Figure of Innocence: Child Pornography Legislation and the Queerness of Childhood," *Quarterly Journal of Speech* 105, no. 3 (2019): 258.

34. Christchurch assailant, "The Great Replacement," 2.

35. Christchurch assailant, "The Great Replacement," 4, capitalization is in the original.

36. Christchurch assailant, "The Great Replacement," 9.

37. See Jacques Lacan, *The Seminar of Jacques Lacan: On Feminine Sexuality, the Limits of Love and Knowledge*, ed. Jacques-Alain Miller and Bruce Fink (New York: Norton, 1999); and Lacan, *The Seminar of Jacques Lacan: Book 1, Freud's Papers on Technique, 1953–1954*, ed. Jacques-Alain Miller, trans. John Forrester (New York: Norton, 1991), 142.

38. El Paso assailant, "The Inconvenient Truth," paragraph 6.

39. Buffalo assailant, "You Wait for a Signal While Your People Wait for You," 2.

40. Bratislava assailant, quoted in Saddiq Basha, "Bratislava Shooting: The Making of Terrorgram's First 'Saint'—RSIS," RSIS Commentary (website), S. Rajartnam School of International Studies, Dec. 21, 2022.

41. For this observation, we are indebted to the research of E. Chebrolu, who documents the ways in which /pol/ rhetoric between white nationalists is organized around rivalrous "banter" and "tough love" for the purpose of correcting behaviors and attitudes that are not sufficiently desirous and protective of whiteness. See Cherbolu's doctoral dissertation, E. Chebrolu, "Modular Whiteness: A Rhetorical Analysis of Racial Anxiety and the Imageboard Vernacular of 4chan's /pol/," D-Scholarship (website), University of Pittsburgh, May 11, 2023, accessed Feb. 6, 2024.

42. Christchurch assailant, "The Great Replacement," 3.

43. Buffalo assailant, "You Wait for a Signal," 1.

44. Bederman, *Manliness and Civilization*, 200. See also E. Cram, *Violent Inheritance: Sexuality, Land, and Energy in Making the North American West* (Berkeley: University of California Press, 2022).

45. Barbara Spackman, *Fascist Virilities: Rhetoric, Ideology, and Social Fantasy in Italy* (Minneapolis: University of Minnesota Press, 1996).

46. Buffalo assailant, "You Wait for a Signal," 4.

47. El Paso assailant, "The Inconvenient Truth," paragraph 4.

48. Christchurch assailant, "The Great Replacement," 4.

49. Christchurch assailant, "The Great Replacement," 35.

50. Poway Synagogue assailant, "An Open Letter," 2.

51. Christchurch assailant, "The Great Replacement," 34.

52. Jacques Lacan, *Écrits: A Selection*, trans. by Bruce Fink (New York: Norton, 2004), 299.

53. Joshua Gunn, "Father Trouble: Staging Sovereignty in Spielberg's *War of the Worlds*," *Critical Studies in Media Communication* 25, no. 1 (2008): 1–27.

54. Here we reference the work of critical race scholars, including but not limited to Charles W. Mills, *The Racial Contract* (Ithaca. NY: Cornell University Press, 1999); Weheliye, *Habeas Viscus*; Hartman, *Scenes of Subjection*; Warren, *Ontological Terror*.

55. Slavoj Žižek, *The Ticklish Subject: The Absent Centre of Political Ontology* (New York: Verso, 2000) 362.

56. See Hawley, *Making Sense of the Alt-Right*; and Niko Heikkilä, "Online Antagonism of the Alt-Right in the 2016 Election," *European Journal of American Studies* 12, no. 12–2 (2017).

57. El Paso assailant, "The Inconvenient Truth," paragraph 2.

58. Christchurch assailant, "The Great Replacement," 5.

59. See Stephanie L Hartzell, "Alt-White: Conceptualizing the 'Alt-Right' as a Rhetorical Bridge between White Nationalism and Mainstream Public Discourse," *Journal of Contemporary Rhetoric* 8, no. 1/2 (2018): 6–25.

60. Christchurch assailant, "The Great Replacement," 37.

61. See Frank B. Wilderson III, *Afropessimism* (New York: Liveright, 2020); Fred Moten, *Stolen Life* (Durham, NC: Duke University Press, 2018); Moon-Kie Jung and João H. Costa Vargas, "Antiblackness of the Social and the Human," in *Antiblackness*, ed. Moon-Kie Jung and João H. Costa Vargas, 1–16 (Durham, NC: Duke University Press, 2021).

62. Christchurch assailant, "The Great Replacement," 10.

63. Christchurch assailant, "The Great Replacement," 46.

64. Christchurch assailant, "The Great Replacement," 37.

65. Christchurch assailant, "The Great Replacement," 22.

66. Christchurch assailant, "The Great Replacement," 37.

67. Christchurch assailant, "The Great Replacement," 21.

68. Christchurch assailant, "The Great Replacement," 14.

69. El Paso assailant, "The Inconvenient Truth," paragraph 6.

70. See Sexton, *Amalgamation Schemes*.

71. Christchurch assailant, "The Great Replacement," 14.

72. Richard Dyer, *White: Essays on Race and Culture* (New York: Routledge, 1997).

73. See also Casey Ryan Kelly, "Donald J. Trump and the Rhetoric of White Ambivalence," *Rhetoric and Public Affairs*, 23, no. 2 (2020), 195–223.

74. Christchurch assailant, "The Great Replacement," 14.

75. Christchurch assailant, "The Great Replacement," 31.

76. Christchurch assailant, "The Great Replacement," 32.

77. Christchurch assailant, "The Great Replacement," 7.

78. Lee Edelman, *No Future: Queer Theory and the Death Drive* (Durham, NC: Duke University Press, 2004), 10.

79. Edelman, *No Future*, 8.

80. Edelman, *No Future*, 10.

81. Christchurch assailant, "The Great Replacement," 41.

82. Edelman, *No Future*, 27.

83. Christchurch assailant, "The Great Replacement," 51.

84. Christchurch assailant, "The Great Replacement," 53.

85. Christchurch assailant, "The Great Replacement," 22.

86. Christchurch assailant, "The Great Replacement," 35.

87. Hatewatch Staff, "Flags and Other Symbols Used by Far-Right Groups in Charlottesville," Southern Poverty Law Center (website), Aug. 12, 2017, accessed Feb. 6, 2024.

88. Thomas K. Nakayama, "Whiteness Is Not Contained," *Communication and Critical/Cultural Studies*, 17, no. 2 (June 8, 2020): 199–201.

89. Myra Washington, "Woke Skin, White Masks: Race and Communication Studies," *Communication and Critical/Cultural Studies*, 17, no. 2 (June 15, 2020): 261–66.

90. Nakayama, "Whiteness Is Not Contained," 3.

91. Hall, *The Fateful Triangle*, 17.

92. See Charles Wade Mills, *Black Rights/White Wrongs: The Critique of Racial Liberalism* (New York: Oxford University Press, 2017).

Chapter 2

1. Christchurch assailant, "The Great Replacement," 6.

2. Casey Ryan Kelly, *Caught on Tape: White Masculinity and Obscene Enjoyment* (London: Oxford University Press 2023). See also Frida Beckman, "Paranoid Masculinity, Or, Toward A New Identity Politics," *Symplokē* 29, no. 1–2 (2021): 235–46; Hamilton Carroll, *Affirmative Reaction: New Formations of White Masculinity* (Durham, NC: Duke University Press, 2011); Paul Elliott Johnson, "Walter White(Ness) Lashes out: Breaking Bad and Male Victimage," *Critical Studies in Media Communication* 34, no. 1 (Mar. 2017): 14–28; Nicholas S. Paliewicz and Emma Frances Bloomfield, "Of Markets, Masks, and (White) Men: Mimetic Performances of Parasitic Publicity During the COVID-19 Pandemic," *Women's Studies in Communication* 46, no. 1 (2023): 65–86; and Josh

Smicker, "COVID-19 and 'Crisis as Ordinary': Pathological Whiteness, Popular Pessimism, and Pre-Apocalyptic Cultural Studies," *Cultural Studies* 35, no. 2–3 (May 4, 2021): 291–305.

3. Richard Slotkin, *Regeneration Through Violence: The Mythology of the American Frontier, 1600–1860* (Norman: University of Oklahoma Press, 2000).

4. See Sally Robinson, *Authenticity Guaranteed: Masculinity and the Rhetoric of Anti-Consumerism in American Culture* (Amherst: University of Massachusetts Press, 2018); Joshua Gunn and Thomas Frentz, "Fighting for Father: *Fight Club* as Cinematic Psychosis," *Western Journal of Communication* 74, no. 3 (May 26, 2010): 269–91; Claire Sisco King, "It Cuts Both Ways: *Fight Club*, Masculinity, and Abject Hegemony," *Communication & Critical/Cultural Studies* 6, no. 4 (Dec. 2009): 366–85.

5. Žižek, *The Ticklish Subject*; Jodi Dean, *Publicity's Secret: How Technoculture Capitalizes on Democracy* (Ithaca, NY: Cornell University Press, 2002).

6. Gunn, "On Political Perversion."

7. Amanda D. Lotz, *Cable Guys: Television and Masculinities in the 21st Century* (New York: New York University Press, 2014).

8. Jason Mittell, *Complex TV: The Poetics of Contemporary Television Storytelling* (New York: New York University Press, 2015), 142–43.

9. Yael Levy, *Chick TV: Antiheroines and Time Unbound* (Syracuse, NY: Syracuse University Press, 2022), 11.

10. Paul du Gay, "Organizing Identity: Entrepreneurial Governance and Public Management," in *Questions of Cultural Identity*, ed. Stuart Hall and Paul du Gay (Thousand Oaks, CA: Sage, 1996), 151–69.

11. Jack Bratich and Sarah Banet-Weiser, "From Pick-Up Artists to Incels: Con(Fidence) Games, Networked Misogyny, and the Failure of Neoliberalism," *International Journal of Communication* 13 (2019): 5003–27.

12. Jodi Melamed, *Represent and Destroy: Rationalizing Violence in the New Racial Capitalism* (Minneapolis: University of Minnesota Press, 2011).

13. Sayak Valencia, *Gore Capitalism* (Cambridge, MA: MIT Press, 2018), 64.

14. Valencia, *Gore Capitalism*, 126.

15. Andrea Cornwall, "Introduction: Masculinities under Neoliberalism," in *Masculinities under Neoliberalism*, ed. Andrea Cornwall (London: Bloomsbury, 2016), 1–28; William Davies, *The Limits of Neoliberalism: Authority, Sovereignty and the Logic of Competition* (Thousand Oaks, CA: Sage, 2016); Henry A. Giroux, "Beyond the Biopolitics of Disposability: Rethinking Neoliberalism in the New Gilded Age," *Social Identities* 14, no. 5 (Sept. 1, 2008): 587–620; Adam Kotsko, "Neoliberalism's Demons," *Theory & Event* 20, no. 2 (2017): 493–509.

16. Shahbaz Khayambashi, "Blood and Guts in Living Color: A Study of the Internet Death Video Community," *OMEGA—Journal of Death and Dying* 83, no. 3 (Aug. 1, 2021): 390–406.

17. Hillary Beaumont, "Inside the World of Columbine-Obsessed Tumblr Bloggers," *Vice* (website), Feb. 24, 2015, accessed Feb. 6, 2024.

18. Valencia, *Gore Capitalism*, 229.

19. David Harvey, "Neoliberalism as Creative Destruction," *Annals of the American Academy of Political and Social Science* 610 (2007): 22–44; Wendy Brown, *In the Ruins of Neoliberalism: The Rise of Antidemocratic Politics in the West* (New York: Columbia University Press, 2019).

20. Brown, *In the Ruins of Neoliberalism*, 171.

21. Christchurch assailant, "The Great Replacement," 30.

22. See Robinson, *Authenticity Guaranteed*, 133–54. In Robinson's analysis of *Fight Club*, she observes how the film takes up Susan Faludi's observation that postwar white masculinity had become ornamental, or more akin to style and performance than a trait associated with essential skills and forms of work. The salaried office worker, the so-called organizational man, no longer produced anything, and new forms of work detached men from the inherent masculinity associated with craft labor. See Susan Faludi, *Stiffed: The Betrayal of the American Man* (New York: Harper Perennial, 2000).

23. Christchurch assailant, "The Great Replacement," 34.

24. Bederman, *Manliness and Civilization*.

25. Christchurch assailant, "The Great Replacement," 34.

26. Christchurch assailant, "The Great Replacement," 19.

27. See Ore, *Lynching*.

28. Christchurch assailant, "The Great Replacement" 53.

29. El Paso assailant, "The Inconvenient Truth," para. 7.

30. See Hannah Arendt, *The Origins of Totalitarianism* (New York: Harcourt, Brace, Jovanovich, 1973); and Hannah Arendt, *On Violence* (Boston: Mariner, 1970).

31. Christchurch assailant, "The Great Replacement," 21.

32. Claire Sisco King argues that the sacrificial (white) man is the ideal citizen-subject of much of contemporary cinema. She contends that films mediate cultural trauma through allegories of sacrifice and redemption through masculine violence. Traumatic heroism becomes a marker of the male citizen-subject's worth. These films illustrate how broader cultural tropes associated with trauma articulate, negotiate, and regulate hegemonic expectations about masculinity, national identity, and civic duty. In this context, white men appropriate cultural trauma to recenter public culture around their feelings of aggrievement. See Claire Sisco King, *Washed in Blood: Male Sacrifice, Trauma, and the Cinema* (New Brunswick, NJ: Rutgers University Press, 2011).

33. Poway Synagogue assailant, "An Open Letter," 3.

34. Populism is a political logic grounded in the tropological resonance of "the people" and "common sense." Conservative populism, in particular, is

often organized around an apocalyptic confrontation between the virtuous people, or everyday folks, and "fat cats" and power brokers who have dispossessed "the people" of the fruits of their hard labor. Conservative populism is enacted through constant antagonism: "the people" (whoever they are) are virtuous (common-sense, simple, god-fearing, hardworking), and their enemies are globalists, elitists, experts, the rich (only some), foreigners, institutions, politicians, and so on. "The people" is a rhetorical construct, meaning that "the people" are invented in discourse, hailed by political mythology that gives them legitimacy to be at the center of US political discourse and in whose name their leaders seek to govern. See Johnson, *I, the People*; Michael J. Lee, "The Populist Chameleon: The People's Party, Huey Long, George Wallace, and the Populist Argumentative Frame," *Quarterly Journal of Speech* 92, no. 4 (Nov. 2006): 355–78; Michael C. McGee, "In Search of 'the People': A Rhetorical Alternative," *Quarterly Journal of Speech* 61, no. 3 (Oct. 1, 1975): 235–49.

35. Christchurch assailant, "The Great Replacement," 5.

36. Poway Synagogue assailant, "An Open Letter," 3.

37. Poway Synagogue assailant, "An Open Letter," 3.

38. El Paso assailant, "The Inconvenient Truth," paragraph 1.

39. Buffalo assailant, "You Wait for a Signal," 3.

40. El Paso assailant, "The Inconvenient Truth," paragraph 7.

41. Umpqua Community College assailant, "My Story," 3.

42. On thanatapolitics, see Stuart Murray, "Thanatopolitics: Reading in Agamben a Rejoinder to Biopolitical Life," *Communication & Critical/Cultural Studies* 5, no. 2 (2008): 203–7; and Stuart Murray, "Thanatopolitics: On the Use of Death for Mobilizing Political Life," *Polygraph: An International Journal of Politics and Culture* 18 (2006): 191–215.

43. Foucault, for instance, details the forms of regimentation, discipline, and bodily habituation required to produce a solider-subject. See Michel Foucault, *Discipline and Punish: The Birth of the Prison* (New York: Vintage, 1977).

44. Christchurch assailant, "The Great Replacement," 53.

45. Debbie Ging, "Alphas, Betas, and Incels: Theorizing the Masculinities of the Manosphere," *Men and Masculinities* 22, no. 4 (Oct. 1, 2019): 638–57; Shawn P. Van Valkenburgh, "Digesting the Red Pill: Masculinity and Neoliberalism in the Manosphere," *Men and Masculinities* 24, no. 1 (Apr. 1, 2021): 84–103.

46. Theodor Adorno et al., *The Authoritarian Personality* (New York: Verso, 2019).

47. Brendan Joel Kelley, "'White Sharia' and Militant White Nationalism," Southern Poverty Law Center (website), Nov. 27, 2017, accessed Feb. 6, 2024.

48. Christchurch assailant, "The Great Replacement," 53.

49. The Red Pill and the Blue Pill are metaphors drawn from the 1999 film

The Matrix, in which the protagonist (Neo) is offered the choice between taking one pill (blue) that will compel him to accept his current reality and another (red) that would awaken him to the real world, in which the earth has been eviscerated and humans are enslaved by machines. These terms were later adopted within the so-called "mansophere," digital ecologies organized around men's rights and antifeminism in order to name the belief that men have been conditioned to accept feminist and multicultural brainwashing. Taking the Red Pill is a metaphor to awakening to this bleak reality and resisting it for masculine empowerment.

50. Christchurch assailant, "The Great Replacement," 20.

51. I borrow this phrase from Judith Butler, *Frames of War: When Is Life Grievable?* (New York: Verso, 2016).

52. Christchurch assailant, "The Great Replacement," 42.

53. El Paso assailant, "The Inconvenient Truth," paragraph 7.

54. El Paso assailant, "The Inconvenient Truth," paragraph 7.

55. Umpqua Community College assailant, "My Story," 2.

56. See James William Gibson, *Warrior Dreams: Violence and Manhood in Post-Vietnam America* (New York: Hill & Wang, 1994).

57. Christchurch assailant, "The Great Replacement," 42; See also Walter Leitsch, "The Siege of Vienna: 1683's Winners and Losers," *History Today* (website), 33 no. 7 (July 7, 1983), accessed Feb. 6, 2024.

58. Christchurch assailant, "The Great Replacement," 73; Buffalo assailant, "You Wait for a Signal," 180.

59. Shannon Weber, "White Supremacy's Old Gods," Political Research Associates (website), Feb. 1, 2018, accessed Feb. 6, 2024.

60. Watts argues that whiteness oftentimes takes on particularity through transcendent discourses of mythology and metaphysics. The white spirit must undergo trials by dark forces to purify and solidify mythic whiteness. He characterizes whiteness as a journey in which the terror of racial impurity must be overcome. This journey is sexual in as much as feminized dark forces threaten to corrupt the vulnerable white body. He writes that "and so, master narratives that pursue mythic whiteness often pit white men against feminized dark forces from within and without the white body as tests of immanent manhood" (191). Eric King Watts, "Border Patrolling and 'Passing' in Eminem's *8 Mile*," *Critical Studies in Media Communication* 22, no. 3 (2005): 187–206.

61. Michael Hyde uses the Greek term *ek-stasis* to denote how the rhetoric of heroism is rooted in acts of "standing outside of and beyond oneself." See Michael J. Hyde, *The Call of Conscience: Heidegger and Levinas, Rhetoric and the Euthanasia Debate* (Columbia: University of South Carolina Press, 2001), 31.

62. Riaz Hassan, *Life as a Weapon: The Global Rise of Suicide Bombings* (Abingdon, UK: Routledge, 2014), 9.

63. Poway Synagogue assailant, "An Open Letter," 5.

64. Samantha Mahood and Halim Rane, "Islamist Narratives in ISIS Recruitment Propaganda," *Journal of International Communication* 23, no. 1 (Jan. 2, 2017): 15–35; Danielle Peled, "ISIS Execution Videos: A Propaganda and Recruitment Tool," *Haaretz* (website), Nov. 17, 2015, accessed Feb. 6, 2024.

65. Christchurch assailant, "The Great Replacement," 39.

66. Slotkin, *Regeneration Through Violence.*

67. Poway Synagogue assailant, "An Open Letter," 8.

68. Poway Synagogue assailant, "An Open Letter," 8.

69. Hasian, "Understanding the Power of Conspiratorial Rhetoric."

70. Poway Synagogue assailant, "An Open Letter," 8.

71. Umpqua Community College assailant, "My Story," 1. We note that this manifesto shares much in common with that of the Isle Vista killer. In that manifesto, the killer expresses the ideology of "incels," or involuntary celibates, who blame women for their inability to have sex or form romantic partnerships. Incels often express violent misogyny and align their politics with fascism. See Casey Ryan Kelly and Chase Aunspach, "Incels, Compulsory Sexuality, and Fascist Masculinity," *Feminist Formations* 32, no. 3 (2020): 145–72.

72. Umpqua Community College assailant, "My Story," 1.

73. Umpqua Community College assailant, "My Story," 1.

74. Joshua Gunn, *Modern Occult Rhetoric: Mass Media and the Drama of Secrecy in the Twentieth Century* (Tuscaloosa: University Alabama Press, 2005).

75. Christchurch assailant, "The Great Replacement," 18.

76. Poway Synagogue assailant, "An Open Letter," 2.

77. Buffalo assailant, "You Wait for a Signal," 9.

78. Poway Synagogue assailant, "An Open Letter," 1.

79. Christchurch assailant, "The Great Replacement," 61.

80. Sara Ahmed illustrates how rhetorics of white supremacy are often built on "love" and fraternity for members of the racial in-group. She writes that "the presence of this other is imagined as a threat to the object of love," thus, love authorizes a relationship of hate and enmity toward the Other. See Ahmed, *Cultural Politics of Emotion*, 43.

81. Judith Butler, *The Force of Nonviolence: The Ethical in the Political (New York: Verso, 2020)*; Judith Butler, *Precarious Life: The Powers of Mourning and Violence* (New York: Verso, 2020).

82. Jasbir K. Puar, *The Right to Maim: Debility, Capacity, Disability* (Durham, NC: Duke University Press, 2017).

83. Butler, *Frames of War,* xxix.

84. See Casey Ryan Kelly, "White Pain," *Quarterly Journal of Speech* 107, no. 2 (Apr. 3, 2021): 209–33; Moten, *Stolen Life*; Weheliye, *Habeas Viscus*; and Wynter, "Unsettling the Coloniality," 257–337.

Chapter 3

1. See Janet Biehl and Peter Staudenmaier, *Ecofascism: Lessons from the German Experience* (Oakland, CA: AK Press, 1995); Sam Moore and Alex Roberts, *The Rise of Ecofascism: Climate Change and the Far Right* (Hoboken, NJ: Wiley, 2022); and Elizabeth Nickson, *Eco-Fascists: How Radical Conservationists Are Destroying Our Natural Heritage* (New York: Harper Collins, 2012).

2. Bernhard Forchtner, *The Far Right and the Environment: Politics, Discourse and Communication* (Abingdon, UK: Routledge, 2019); Pam Nilan, *Young People and the Far Right* (New York: Springer Nature, 2021); Maria-Sophia Quine, *Population Politics in Twentieth Century Europe: Fascist Dictatorships and Liberal Democracies* (Abingdon, UK: Routledge, 2013).

3. Kurt W. Ritter, "American Political Rhetoric and the Jeremiad Tradition: Presidential Nomination Acceptance Addresses, 1960–1976," *Central States Speech Journal* 31, no. 3 (Sept. 1, 1980): 153–57.

4. Chetan Bhatt, "White Extinction: Metaphysical Elements of Contemporary Western Fascism," *Theory, Culture & Society* 38, no. 1 (Jan. 1, 2021): 27–52; Benoît Dillet, "We Haven't Seen Anything Yet . . . : Accelerationism and Decelerationism under Austerity," *Cultural Politics* 11, no. 2 (July 1, 2015): 296–300; Michael Loadenthal, "Feral Fascists and Deep Green Guerrillas: Infrastructural Attack and Accelerationist Terror," *Critical Studies on Terrorism* 15, no. 1 (Jan. 2, 2022): 169–208; and Imogen Richards, Callum Jones, and Gearóid Brinn, "Eco-Fascism Online: Conceptualizing Far-Right Actors' Response to Climate Change on Stormfront," *Studies in Conflict & Terrorism* (online first Dec. 18, 2022): 1–27.

5. Zachary Kamel, Mack Lamoureux, and Ben Makuch, "'Eco-Fascist' Arm of Neo-Nazi Terror Group, The Base, Linked to Swedish Arson," *Vice* (website), Jan. 29, 2020, accessed Feb. 6, 2024.

6. El Paso assailant, "The Inconvenient Truth," paragraph 6.

7. El Paso assailant, "The Inconvenient Truth," para. 3.

8. Ritter, "American Political Rhetoric and the Jeremiad Tradition."

9. Sacvan Bercovitch, *The American Jeremiad* (Madison: University of Wisconsin Press, 1978).

10. Bercovitch, *The American Jeremiad*, 75.

11. Daniel O. Buehler, "Permanence and Change in Theodore Roosevelt's Conservation Jeremiad," *Western Journal of Communication* 62, no. 4 (Dec. 1, 1998): 443.

12. Winthrop D. Jordan, *White Over Black: American Attitudes toward the Negro, 1550–1812,* 2nd ed. (Chapel Hill: University of North Carolina Press, 2012), 297.

13. Katherine Henry, "'Slaves to a Debt': Race, Shame, and the Anti-Obama Jeremiad," *Quarterly Journal of Speech* 100, no. 3 (Aug. 2014): 303–22; John M.

Murphy, "'A Time of Shame and Sorrow': Robert F. Kennedy and the American Jeremiad," *Quarterly Journal of Speech* 76, no. 4 (Nov. 1, 1990): 401–14.

14. Buehler, "Permanence and Change," 450.

15. See Dorsey, *We Are All Americans, Pure and Simple*; Leroy G. Dorsey, "The Frontier Myth in Presidential Rhetoric: Theodore Roosevelt's Campaign for Conservation," *Western Journal of Communication* 59, no. 1 (Mar. 1, 1995): 1–19.

16. Michael Cobb, *God Hates Fags: The Rhetorics of Religious Violence* (New York: New York University Press, 2006); Richard L. Johannesen, "Ronald Reagan's Economic Jeremiad," *Central States Speech Journal* 37, no. 2 (June 1, 1986): 79–89.

17. Henry, "Slaves to Debt."

18. James Sayer and Norbert H. Mills, "The Jeremiadic Rhetoric of the Political Right," *Florida Communication Journal*, 29, no. 2 (2001): 58–65.

19. Michelle Rodino-Colocino, "Geek Jeremiads: Speaking the Crisis of Job Loss by Opposing Offshored and H-1B Labor," *Communication & Critical/Cultural Studies* 9, no. 1 (Mar. 2012): 22–46.

20. Christchurch assailant, "The Great Replacement," 10.

21. Christchurch assailant, "The Great Replacement," 17.

22. Buffalo assailant, "You Wait for a Signal," 5.

23. Christchurch assailant, "The Great Replacement," 1.

24. Christchurch assailant, "The Great Replacement," 1.

25. Christchurch assailant, "The Great Replacement," 1.

26. Christchurch assailant, "The Great Replacement," 3.

27. El Paso assailant, "The Inconvenient Truth," paragraph 1.

28. Christchurch assailant, "The Great Replacement," 22.

29. Buffalo assailant, "You Wait for a Signal," 51.

30. Cisneros, "Contaminated Communities."

31. Buffalo assailant, "You Wait for a Signal," 1.

32. Christchurch assailant, "The Great Replacement," 4.

33. El Paso assailant, "The Inconvenient Truth," paragraph 1.

34. El Paso assailant, "The Inconvenient Truth," paragraph 4.

35. Buffalo assailant, "You Wait for a Signal," 7.

36. Buffalo assailant, "You Wait for a Signal," 51.

37. Christchurch assailant, "The Great Replacement," 6.

38. Oslo assailant, "2083: A European Declaration of Independence."

39. Christchurch assailant, "The Great Replacement," 6.

40. Buffalo assailant, "You Wait for a Signal," 6.

41. Buffalo assailant, "You Wait for a Signal," 6.

42. Christchurch assailant, "The Great Replacement," 6.

43. Christchurch assailant, "The Great Replacement," 6.

44. Christchurch assailant, "The Great Replacement," 70. All caps in the original.

45. El Paso assailant, "The Inconvenient Truth," paragraph 3.

46. Christchurch assailant, "The Great Replacement," 22.

47. Christchurch assailant, "The Great Replacement," 22.

48. See Cisneros, "Contaminated Communities."

49. Oslo assailant, "2083: A European declaration of independence," 5.

50. Christchurch assailant, "The Great Replacement," 5.

51. El Paso assailant, "The Inconvenient Truth," paragraph 5.

52. Christchurch assailant, "The Great Replacement," 6.

53. Christchurch assailant, "The Great Replacement," 24.

54. While any serious study of history would disentangle "democratic" from "peaceful," ecofascists regard democracy as an inherently passive and ineffective means of maintaining white supremacy.

55. El Paso assailant, "The Inconvenient Truth," paragraph 2.

56. Christchurch assailant, "The Great Replacement," 6.

57. Christchurch assailant, "The Great Replacement," 34.

58. Christchurch assailant, "The Great Replacement," 45.

59. Christchurch assailant, "The Great Replacement," 6.

60. Christchurch assailant, "The Great Replacement," 45.

61. Buffalo assailant, "You Wait for a Signal," 6.

62. Christchurch assailant, "The Great Replacement," 39.

Chapter 4

1. Graham Macklin, "The Cumulative Momentum of Transnational Extreme-Right Terrorism," in *A Transnational History of Right-Wing Terrorism,* ed. Johannes Dafinger and Moritz Florin (Abingdon, UK: Routledge, 2022); Stephane J. Baele, Lewys Brace, and Travis G. Coan, "From 'Incel' to 'Saint': Analyzing the Violent Worldview behind the 2018 Toronto Attack," *Terrorism and Political Violence* 33, no. 8 (Aug. 2, 2019): 1–25; Saddiq Basha, "Bratislava Shooting: The Making of Terrorgram's First 'Saint'—RSIS," RSIS Commentary (website), S. Rajartnam School of International Studies, Dec. 21, 2022, accessed Feb. 6, 2024; "Revered as a Saint by Online Extremists, How the Christchurch Shooter Inspired Copycat Terrorists around the World," *The Independent* (website), Aug. 24, 2019, accessed Feb. 6, 2024; Stassa Edwards, "Saint Elliot Rodger and the 'Incels' Who Canonize Him," Jezebel (website), Apr. 27, 2018, accessed Feb. 6, 2024.

2. Matthew Kriner, "Analysing Terrorgram Publications: A New Digital Zine," Global Network on Extremism & Technology (website), Sept. 12, 2022, accessed Feb. 6, 2024.

3. Hannah Gais and Megan Squire, "How an Encrypted Messaging Platform

Is Changing Extremist Movements," Southern Poverty Law Center (website), Feb. 16, 2021, accessed Feb. 6, 2024.

4. Kyle R. Larson and George F. (Guy) McHendry. "Parasitic Publics." *Rhetoric Society Quarterly* 49, no. 5 (Oct. 20, 2019): 517–41.

5. Kirt H. Wilson, "The Racial Politics of Imitation in the Nineteenth Century," *Quarterly Journal of Speech* 89, no. 2 (May 2003): 89–108.

6. Michele Kennerly and Damien Smith Pfister. "Poiēsis, Genesis, Mimēsis: Toward a Less Selfish Genealogy of Memes," in *Ancient Rhetorics and Digital Networks*, ed. Michele Kennerly and Damien Smith Pfister, 205–28 (Tuscaloosa: University of Alabama Press, 2018), 208.

7. Kennerly and Pfister, "Poiēsis, Genesis, Mimēsis," 222.

8. For instance, see Jonathan Franklin, "Parts of the Buffalo Shooter's Alleged Screed Were Copied from Other Sources," *NPR* (website), May 18, 2022, accessed Feb. 6, 2024.

9. Christchurch assailant, "The Great Replacement," 2.

10. Christchurch assailant, "The Great Replacement," 1.

11. Bratislava assailant, quoted in Basha, "Bratislava Shooting."

12. Lane quoted in Kaplan, *Encyclopedia of White Power*, 167.

13. Michael J. Preston, "Traditional Humor from the Fax Machine: 'All of a Kind,'" *Western Folklore* 53, no. 2 (1994): 147–69.

14. Michael Warner, "Publics and Counterpublics (Abbreviated Version)," *Quarterly Journal of Speech* 88, no. 4 (Nov. 1, 2002): 413–25.

15. See Henry Jenkins, Sam Ford, and Joshua Green, *Spreadable Media: Creating Value and Meaning in a Networked Culture* (New York: New York University Press, 2013); and Henry Jenkins, *Convergence Culture: Where Old and New Media Collide* (New York: New York University Press, 2008).

16. Robert Topinka, "The Politics of Anti-Discourse: Copypasta, the Alt-Right, and the Rhetoric of Form," *Theory & Event* 25, no. 2 (Apr. 2022): 392–418.

17. Topinka, "The Politics of Anti-Discourse," 393.

18. Topinka, "The Politics of Anti-Discourse," 395.

19. Gunn, "Maranatha," 364.

20. Slavoj Žižek, *Looking Awry: An Introduction to Jacques Lacan Through Popular Culture* (Cambridge, MA: MIT Press, 1992), 53.

21. Žižek, *Looking Awry*, 53.

22. For more on signifying under conditions of "failed unicity," see Lundberg, *Lacan in Public.*

23. Žižek, *Looking Awry*, 55.

24. Žižek, *Looking Awry*, 55.

25. Christchurch assailant, "The Great Replacement," 20.

26. "Navy Seal Copypasta," Know Your Meme (website), accessed May 18, 2020.

27. Robert Evans, cited in Aja Romano, "How the Christchurch Shooter Used Memes to Spread Hate," *Vox* (website), Mar. 16, 2019, accessed Feb. 6, 2024.

28. Garth S. Jowett and Victoria O'Donnell, *Propaganda and Persuasion* (Thousand Oaks, CA: Sage, 2011).

29. Walter Benjamin, *The Work of Art in the Age of Mechanical Reproduction* (London: Penguin, 2008), 245.

30. See Nathan Crick, ed., *The Rhetoric of Fascism* (Tuscaloosa: University of Alabama Press, 2022); Bradford Vivian, "The Incitement: An Account of Language, Power, and Fascism," *Rhetoric Society Quarterly* 51, no. 5 (Oct. 20, 2021): 361–76.

31. Theodor W. Adorno, *Aspects of the New Right-Wing Extremism* (Hoboken, NJ: Wiley, 2020), 13.

32. Adorno, *Aspects of the New Right-Wing Extremism*, 30.

33. Adorno, *Aspects of the New Right-Wing Extremism*, 30.

34. Herbert Marcuse, *The Aesthetic Dimension: Toward a Critique of Marxist Aesthetics* (Boston: Beacon Press, 1978), 51.

35. Marcuse, *The Aesthetic Dimension*, 52.

36. See also Wilhelm Reich, *The Mass Psychology of Fascism*, 3rd edition, trans. Vincent R. Carfagno (New York: Farrar, Straus, and Giroux, 1980). See also Umberto Eco, "Eternal Fascism: Fourteen Ways of Looking at a Blackshirt," *New York Review of Books*, June 22, 1995.

37. See Joshua Gunn, "Gunplay," Carroll C. Arnold Distinguished Lecture, National Communications Association (website), Nov. 9, 2018, accessed Feb. 6, 2024.

38. Phillips and Milner, *You Are Here*.

39. See Calum Lister Matheson, "Liberal Tears and the Rogue's Yarn of Sadistic Conservativism," *Rhetoric Society Quarterly* 52, no. 4 (Aug. 8, 2022): 341–55; and Alaina Walberg, "Owning the Libs: Symbolic Negation of #mybodymychoice as a Conservative Rhetorical Strategy," *Communication Studies* (online first Jan. 9, 2023): 1–16.

40. Buffalo assailant, "You Wait on a Signal," 61.

41. Wayne C. Booth, *A Rhetoric of Irony* (Chicago: University of Chicago Press, 1974); Kenneth Burke, *A Grammar of Motives* (Berkeley: University of California Press, 1969).

42. Dana Cloud, "The Irony Bribe and Reality Television: Investment and Detachment in *The Bachelor*," *Critical Studies in Media Communication* 27, no. 5 (Dec. 2010): 413–37; See also Michelle Colpean and Meg Tully, "Not Just a Joke: Tina Fey, Amy Schumer, and the Weak Reflexivity of White Feminist Comedy," *Women's Studies in Communication* 42, no. 2 (Apr. 3, 2019): 161–80.

43. Helene A. Shugart, "Postmodern Irony as Subversive Rhetorical Strategy," *Western Journal of Communication* 63, no. 4 (Fall 1999): 436.

44. See Burke, *Attitudes Toward History.*

45. Christchurch assailant, "The Great Replacement," 4.

46. Rumi Khan, "The Alt-Right as Counterculture: Memes, Videogames and Violence," Harvard Political Review (website), July 6, 2019, accessed Feb. 6, 2024.

47. Christchurch assailant, "The Great Replacement," 17.

48. See Matt Lees, "What Gamergate Should Have Taught Us about the 'Alt-Right,'" *The Guardian* (website), Dec. 1, 2016, accessed Feb. 6, 2024. John Michael Colón, "Beta Testing Fascism: How Online Culture Wars Created the Alt-Right," *In These Times* (website), June 27, 2017, accessed Feb. 6, 2024.

49. Anastasia Salter and Bridget Blodgett, *Toxic Geek Masculinity in Media: Sexism, Trolling, and Identity Policing* (New York: Palgrave Macmillan, 2017).

50. See Nagle, *Kill All Normies.*

51. Meilan Solly, "Before Chain Letters Swept the Internet, They Raised Funds for Orphans and Sent Messages from God," *Smithsonian Magazine* (website), July 2, 2020, accessed Feb. 6, 2024.

52. Poway Synagogue assailant, "An Open Letter," 4.

53. See Joshua Gunn and Dana L. Cloud, "Agentic Orientation as Magical Voluntarism," *Communication Theory* 20, no. 1 (2010): 50–78.

54. See chapter 2 in Kelly, *Apocalypse Man.*

55. "Slender Man Stabbing: Girl Gets 25 Years in Mental Hospital," *BBC News* (website), Dec. 21, 2017, accessed Feb. 6, 2024.

56. Merrit Kennedy, "'Pizzagate' Gunman Sentenced To 4 Years In Prison," *NPR* (website), June 22, 2017, accessed Feb. 6, 2024.

57. We borrow "reality referencing" from Mary E. Triece, who coined the term to denote the rhetorical resources recipients derive from their own experience to test discourse that belies material reality. See Mary E. Triece, "'Saying It the Way We Have Lived It': Pragmatics and the 'Impossible Position' of Ideology Critique," *Western Journal of Communication* 75, no. 4 (July 2011): 434–39.

58. Miller-Idriss, *Hate in the Homeland.*

59. The work on political pranking tends to emphasize the transformative potential of practices such as "culture jamming," detournément, and other forms of transgression that appropriate and subvert dominant messages. The far-right, however, has adopted these traditionally left-leaning approaches to portray itself as a mischievous counterculture rather than a staunchly fascist political movement. Though it is beyond the scope of this chapter, it is worth considering how the far-right appropriates and subverts leftist political rhetoric and performances. See Christine Harold, "Pranking Rhetoric: 'Culture Jamming' as Media Activism," *Critical Studies in Media Communication* 21, no. 3 (Sept. 2004): 189–211; Kembrew McLeod, *Pranksters: Making Mischief in the Modern World* (New York: New York University Press, 2014).

60. Phillips and Milner, *The Ambivalent Internet*, 112.

61. Poway Synagogue assailant, "An Open Letter," 7.

62. "Moon Man," Anti-Defamation League (website), accessed Feb. 18, 2023.

63. Poway Synagogue assailant, "An Open Letter," 8.

64. Randall A. Lake, "Enacting Red Power: The Consummatory Function in Native American Protest Rhetoric," *Quarterly Journal of Speech* 69, no. 2 (May 1983): 127.

65. Poway Synagogue assailant, "An Open Letter," 5.

66. Damien Smith Pfister, "The Logos of the Blogosphere: Flooding the Zone, Invention, and Attention in the Lott Imbroglio," *Argumentation and Advocacy* 47, no. 3 (Jan. 1, 2011): 141–62.

67. Brian Stelter, "This Infamous Steve Bannon Quote Is Key to Understanding America's Crazy Politics," *CNN* (website), Nov. 16, 2021, accessed Feb. 7, 2024.

68. Smicker, "COVID-19 and 'Crisis as Ordinary,'" 299.

69. Douglas Kellner, *Guys and Guns Amok: Domestic Terrorism and School Shootings from the Oklahoma City Bombing to the Virginia Tech Massacre* (Abingdon, UK: Routledge, 2008), 91.

70. David Schmid, *Natural Born Celebrities: Serial Killers in American Culture* (Chicago: University of Chicago Press, 2006).

71. Bryan J. McCann, "Duplicity and the Depraved Uncanny in Mediations of Ted Bundy," *Women's Studies in Communication* 44, no. 3 (2021): 340–59.

72. Joshua Gamson, "The Unwatched Life Is Not Worth Living: The Elevation of the Ordinary in Celebrity Culture." *PMLA* 126 no. 4 (2011): 1061–69.

73. Alice E. Marwick, *Status Update: Celebrity, Publicity, and Branding in the Social Media Age* (New Haven, CT: Yale University Press, 2015), 15–16.

74. Alice E. Marwick, "You May Know Me from YouTube: (Micro-)Celebrity in Social Media," in *A Companion to Celebrity*, ed. P. David Marshall and Sean Redmond (Wiley, 2015).

75. Umpqua Community College assailant, "My Story," 3.

76. Poway Synagogue assailant, "An Open Letter," 8.

77. Buffalo assailant, "You Wait for a Signal," 3.

78. Fruzsina Eordogh, "How 4chan Tricked the Internet into Believing This Comedian Is a Mass Shooter," *Forbes* (website), June 2, 2016, accessed Feb. 7, 2024.

79. Umpqua Community College assailant, "My Story," 4.

80. Poway Synagogue assailant, "An Open Letter," 7.

81. Buffalo assailant, "You Wait for a Signal," 10.

82. Alexis C. Madrigal, "AMA: How a Weird Internet Thing Became a Mainstream Delight," *The Atlantic* (website), Jan. 7, 2014, accessed Feb. 7, 2024.

83. See Rebekka Kreling, Adrian Meier, and Leonard Reinecke, "Feeling Authentic on Social Media: Subjective Authenticity across Instagram Stories and Posts," *Social Media + Society* 8, no. 1 (Mar. 24, 2022); and Josie Reade, "Keeping It Raw on the 'gram: Authenticity, Relatability and Digital Intimacy in Fitness Cultures on Instagram," *New Media & Society* 23, no. 3 (Mar. 1, 2021): 535–53.

84. See Robinson, *Authenticity Guaranteed.*

85. Tess Owen, "Meet 4chan's 'Kommandos,' the Armed Meme Lords Driving Gun Culture," *Vice* (website), July 8, 2021, accessed Feb. 7, 2024.

86. Blyth Crawford, "/K/ and the Visual Culture of Weapons Boards," Centre for Research and Evidence on Security Threats (website), Oct. 28, 2020, accessed Feb. 7, 2024.

87. Although the Bratislava assailant included discussions of his armaments like those on /k/, he credited most of his weapons and tactical knowledge to telegram.

88. Buffalo assailant, "You Wait for a Signal," 62. "Gear queer" is an internet slang term for people who collect an extensive amount of weapons and paramilitary gear.

89. El Paso assailant, "The Inconvenient Truth," paragraph 4.

90. Mark Ledwich and Anna Zaitsev, "Algorithmic Extremism: Examining YouTube's Rabbit Hole of Radicalization," *First Monday*, Feb. 26, 2020.

91. Oliver Lee Bateman, "YouTube's Gun Reviewers Are 'Guns & Ammo' Magazine for the Internet Age," *Vice* (website), Mar. 25, 2017, accessed Feb. 7, 2024.

92. Lisa Jordan, James Kalin, and Colleen Dabrowski, "Characteristics of Gun Advertisements on Social Media: Systematic Search and Content Analysis of Twitter and YouTube Posts," *Journal of Medical Internet Research* 22, no. 3 (Mar. 27, 2020).

93. The jargon and euphemisms used on /k/ bear similarity to nuclear planning discourse insofar as both employ specialized terms that shield audiences from the horrific consequences of military weapons. Scholars who have written about "nukespeak" observe how euphemisms and technical language numb listeners and lower the threshold for their usage. See Edward Schiappa, "The Rhetoric of Nukespeak," *Communication Monographs* 56, no. 3 (Sept. 1, 1989): 253–72.

94. This list is by no means exhaustive but represents a cross section of the work on affect and form. See Ahmed, *Cultural Politics of Emotion*; Eugenie Brinkema, *The Forms of the Affects* (Durham, NC: Duke University Press, 2014); Catherine Chaput, "Rhetorical Circulation in Late Capitalism: Neoliberalism and the Overdetermination of Affective Energy," *Philosophy & Rhetoric* 43, no. 1 (Febr. 2010): 1–25; Melissa Gregg and Gregory J. Seigworth, eds., *The Affect Theory Reader* (Durham, NC: Duke University Press, 2010); Brian Massumi,

Parables for the Virtual: Movement, Affect, Sensation (Durham, NC: Duke University Press, 2002); Brian L. Ott, "The Visceral Politics of *V for Vendetta*: On Political Affect in Cinema," *Critical Studies in Media Communication* 27, no. 1 (Mar. 2010): 39–54; Erin J. Rand, "'What One Voice Can Do': Civic Pedagogy and Choric Collectivity at Camp Courage," *Text and Performance Quarterly* 34, no. 1 (Jan. 2, 2014): 28–51; Jenny Edbauer Rice, "The New 'New': Making a Case for Critical Affect Studies," *Quarterly Journal of Speech* 94, no. 2 (May 2008): 200–212.

95. Williams, "Film Bodies."

Epilogue

1. N. Kirkpatrick, Atthar Mirza, and Manuel Canales, "The Blast Effect: How Bullets from an AR-15 Blow the Body Apart," *Washington Post* (website), Mar. 27, 2022, accessed Feb. 7, 2024.

2. Scott Pelley, "What Makes the AR-15 Style Rifle the Weapon of Choice for Mass Shooters?," CBS News (website), May 29, 2022, accessed Feb. 7, 2024.

3. FBI bulletin quoted in Jana Winter, "Texas Mass Shooter Posted Neo-Nazi Content, FBI Document Reveals," *Rolling Stone* (website), May 8, 2023, accessed Feb. 7, 2024.

4. "RWDS/Right Wing Death Squad," Anti-Defamation League (website), May 10, 2023, accessed Feb. 7, 2024.

5. John Knefel, "Right-Wing Media Responded to News That the Allen, Texas, Shooter Is a Neo-Nazi by Calling It a 'Psyop,'" Media Matters for America (website), May 9, 2023, accessed Feb. 7, 2024.

6. Richard Hall, "Elon Musk Appears to Entertain Conspiracy Theory That Texas Shooting Was a 'Psyop,'" *The Independent* (website), May 10, 2023, accessed Feb. 7, 2024; and Chauncey DeVega, "Mass Shootings: America's Slow Civil War," Salon (website), May 9, 2023, accessed Feb. 7, 2024.

7. Center on Extremism, "Murder and Extremism in the United States in 2022" Anti-Defamation League, Feb. 22, 2023, accessed Feb. 7, 2024.

8. Bryn Nelson, "How Stochastic Terrorism Uses Disgust to Incite Violence," *Scientific American* (website), Nov. 5, 2022, accessed Feb. 7, 2024.

9. Many mass killers do not leave behind lengthy manifestos but do make statements that reflected their immersion in hate speech. For instance, the man who killed six Asian American women at an Atlanta area spa told police that he was a sex and pornography addict who chose his targets to "take out that temptation." Although the killer disavowed any racial motivation, his choice of victim reflects long-standing racist assumptions of the hypersexuality and corrupting moral influence of Asian women. His social media accounts also included anti-Asian posts about Chinese responsibility for COVID-19. See Holly Honderich, "Atlanta Spa Shootings: How We Talk about Violence," *BBC News*,

Mar. 19, 2021, https://www.bbc.com/news/world-us-canada-56446820; and Angela R. Gover, Shannon B. Harper, and Lynn Langton, "Anti-Asian Hate Crime During the COVID-19 Pandemic: Exploring the Reproduction of Inequality," *American Journal of Criminal Justice* 45, no. 4 (2020): 647–67.

10. Flores, *Deportable and Disposable*, 57.

11. Flores, *Deportable and Disposable*, 57.

12. Ore, *Lynching*, 33, 45.

13. Beltrán, *Cruelty as Citizenship*, 11, 19.

14. Cheryl I. Harris, "Whiteness as Property," *Harvard Law Review* 106, no. 8 (1993): 1707–91.

15. Karma R. Chávez, *The Borders of AIDS: Race, Quarantine, and Resistance* (Seattle: University of Washington Press, 2021); Michael Lechuga, *Visions of Invasion: Alien Affects, Cinema, and Citizenship in Settler Colonies* (Jackson: University Press of Mississippi, 2023); and Weheliye, *Habeas Viscus*.

16. See Mbembe, *Necropolitics*.

17. See Slavoj Žižek, *Welcome to the Desert of the Real: Five Essays on September 11 and Related Dates* (London: Verso, 2013).

18. McCann, "Duplicity."

19. McCann, "Serial Murder as Modernist Ritual," 53. See also Darrell Y. Hamamoto, "Empire of Death: Militarized Society and the Rise of Serial Killing and Mass Murder," *New Political Science* 24, no. 1 (Mar. 1, 2002): 105–20.

20. Casey Ryan Kelly, "COVID-19 Conspiracy Rhetoric and Other Primal Fantasies," *Quarterly Journal of Speech* 109, no. 2. (May 25, 2023) 132–53; and Mills, *The Racial Contract*.

21. Jeanette Ferrara, "The Psychology of Copycat Crime," *JSTOR Daily* (website), May 11, 2016, accessed Feb. 7, 2024; Adam Lankford, "Do the Media Unintentionally Make Mass Killers into Celebrities? An Assessment of Free Advertising and Earned Media Value," *Celebrity Studies* 9, no. 3 (July 3, 2018): 340–54; Ray Surette, *Copycat Crime and Copycat Criminals* (Boulder, CO: Lynne Rienner Publishers, 2022).

22. Megan Eatman, *Ecologies of Harm: Rhetorics of Violence in the United States* (Columbus: Ohio State University Press, 2020), 4.

23. Jackson, *Scripting the Black Masculine Body*.

24. Hartman, *Scenes of Subjection*; Moten, *Stolen Life*; and Wilderson, *Afropessimism*.

25. Joshua Gunn, "Gunplay," Carroll C. Arnold Distinguished Lecture, National Communication Association (website), Nov. 9, 2018, accessed Feb. 7, 2024.

26. See Laura J. Collins, "The Second Amendment as Demanding Subject: Figuring the Marginalized Subject in Demands for an Unbridled Second Amendment," *Rhetoric & Public Affairs* 17, no. 4 (Winter 2014): 737–56; and

Brett Lunceford, "Armed Victims: The Ego Function of Second Amendment Rhetoric," *Rhetoric & Public Affairs* 18, no. 2 (June 19, 2015): 333–45.

27. E. Chebrolu, "Free Speech and Loss in White Nationalist Rhetoric," *First Amendment Studies* 54, no. 2 (Mar. 2021): 197–208; Casey Ryan Kelly, "Whiteness, Repressive Victimhood, and the Foil of the Intolerant Left," *First Amendment Studies* 55, no. 1 (Jan. 2, 2021): 59–76; and Nadine Strossen, *HATE: Why We Should Resist It With Free Speech, Not Censorship* (New York: Oxford University Press, 2018).

28. Matthew Grady and Rikar Hussein, "White Supremacy Thriving Online, Despite Prevention Efforts," *VOA News* (website), Oct. 30, 2019, accessed Feb. 7, 2024.

29. Rachel Levinson-Waldman, "School Social Media Monitoring Won't Stop the Next Mass Shooting," Tech Policy Press (website), June 22, 2022, accessed Feb. 7, 2024.

30. Sam Levin, "White Supremacists and Militias Have Infiltrated Police across US, Report Says," *The Guardian* (website), Aug. 27, 2020, accessed Feb. 7, 2024.

31. John Drabble, "From White Supremacy to White Power: The FBI, COINTELPRO-WHITEHATE, and the Nazification of the Ku Klux Klan in the 1970s," *American Studies* (Sept. 1, 2007): 49–74.

32. Jens F. Binder and Jonathan Kenyon, "Terrorism and the Internet: How Dangerous Is Online Radicalization?" *Frontiers in Psychology* 13 (Oct. 13, 2022), doi: 10.3389/fpsyg.2022.997390.

33. Billie Murray, *Combating Hate: A Framework for Direct Action* (University Park: Pennsylvania State University Press, 2022).

34. Herbert Marcuse, "Repressive Tolerance," in *A Critique of Pure Tolerance* (Boston: Beacon Press, 1965), 81–123; and Karl Popper, *The Open Society and Its Enemies* (Abingdon, UK: Routledge, 2012). Popper's book was originally published in 1945.

35. Richard Delgado and Jean Stefancic, *Must We Defend Nazis? Hate Speech, Pornography, and the New First Amendment* (New York: New York University Press, 1999).

Selected Bibliography

Adorno, Theodor W. *Aspects of the New Right-Wing Extremism*. Wiley, 2020.

Adorno, Theodor, Else Frenkel-Brunswik, Daniel J. Levinson, and R. Nevitt Sanford. *The Authoritarian Personality*. New York: Verso, 2019.

Ahmed, Sara. *Cultural Politics of Emotion*. Edinburgh: Edinburgh University Press, 2014.

Alcoff, Linda Martín. *The Future of Whiteness*. Cambridge, UK: Polity, 2015.

Anderson, Benedict. *Imagined Communities: Reflections on the Origin and Spread of Nationalism*. New York: Verso, 1991.

Arendt, Hannah. *On Violence*. Mariner Books, 1970.

———. *The Origins of Totalitarianism*. 1st ed. New York: Harcourt, Brace, Jovanovich, 1973.

Balleck, Barry J. *Hate Groups and Extremist Organizations in America: An Encyclopedia*. Santa Barbara, CA: ABC-CLIO, 2019.

Bederman, Gail. *Manliness and Civilization: A Cultural History of Gender and Race in the United States, 1880–1917*. Chicago: University of Chicago Press, 2008.

Belew, Kathleen. *Bring the War Home: The White Power Movement and Paramilitary America*. Cambridge, MA: Harvard University Press, 2019.

Beltrán, Cristina. *Cruelty as Citizenship: How Migrant Suffering Sustains White Democracy*. Minneapolis: University of Minnesota Press, 2020.

Benjamin, Walter. *The Work of Art in the Age of Mechanical Reproduction*. London: Penguin UK, 2008.

Bercovitch, Sacvan. *The American Jeremiad*. Madison: University of Wisconsin Press, 2012.

Berlant, Lauren. *The Queen of America Goes to Washington City: Essays on Sex and Citizenship*. Durham, NC: Duke University Press, 1997.

Bernstein, Robin. *Racial Innocence: Performing American Childhood from Slavery to Civil Rights*. New York: New York University Press, 2011.

Biehl, Janet, and Peter Staudenmaier. *Ecofascism: Lessons from the German Experience*. Oakland, CA: AK Press, 1995.

Bonilla-Silva, Eduardo. *Racism Without Racists: Color-Blind Racism and the*

Persistence of Racial Inequality in the United States. Lanham, MD: Rowman & Littlefield, 2010.

Booth, Wayne C., *A Rhetoric of Irony*. Chicago: University of Chicago Press, 1974.

Brinkema, Eugenie. *The Forms of the Affects*. Durham, NC: Duke University Press, 2014.

Brown, Wendy. *In the Ruins of Neoliberalism: The Rise of Antidemocratic Politics in the West*. New York: Columbia University Press, 2019.

Burke, Kenneth. *Attitudes Toward History*. 3rd ed. Berkeley: University of California Press, 1984.

———. *A Grammar of Motives*. Berkeley: University of California Press, 1969.

———. *The Philosophy of Literary Form*. 3rd ed. Berkeley: University of California Press, 1974.

Butler, Judith. *The Force of Nonviolence: The Ethical in the Political*. New York: Verso, 2020.

———. *Frames of War: When Is Life Grievable?* New York: Verso, 2016.

———. *Precarious Life: The Powers of Mourning and Violence*. New York: Verso, 2020.

Campbell, Karlyn Kohrs, and Kathleen Hall Jamieson. *Form and Genre: Shaping Rhetorical Action*. Falls Church, VA: The Speech Communication Association, 1978.

Carroll, Hamilton. *Affirmative Reaction: New Formations of White Masculinity*. Durham, NC: Duke University Press, 2011.

Chavez, Karma R. *The Borders of AIDS: Race, Quarantine, and Resistance*. Seattle: University of Washington Press, 2021.

———. *Queer Migration Politics: Activist Rhetoric and Coalitional Possibilities*. Urbana: University of Illinois Press, 2013.

Cobb, Michael. *God Hates Fags: The Rhetorics of Religious Violence*. New York: New York University Press, 2006.

Crick, Nathan, ed. *The Rhetoric of Fascism*. Tuscaloosa: University of Alabama Press, 2022.

Curry, Tommy J. *The Man-Not: Race, Class, Genre, and the Dilemmas of Black Manhood*. Philadelphia: Temple University Press, 2017.

Davies, William. *The Limits of Neoliberalism: Authority, Sovereignty and the Logic of Competition*. Thousand Oaks, CA: Sage, 2016.

Dean, Jodi. *Publicity's Secret: How Technoculture Capitalizes on Democracy*. Ithaca, NY: Cornell University Press, 2002.

Delgado, Richard, and Jean Stefancic. *Must We Defend Nazis?: Hate Speech, Pornography, and the New First Amendment*. New York: New York University Press, 1999.

Dorsey, Leroy G. *We Are All Americans, Pure and Simple: Theodore Roosevelt and the Myth of Americanism*. Tuscaloosa: University of Alabama Press, 2013.

Dubrofsky, E. Rachel. *Authenticating Whiteness: Karens, Selfies, and Pop Stars*. Jackson: University Press of Mississippi, 2022.

Dyer, Richard. *White: Essays on Race and Culture*. New York: Routledge, 1997.

Eagleton, Terry. *On Evil*. New Haven, CT.: Yale University Press, 2011.

Eatman, Megan. *Ecologies of Harm: Rhetorics of Violence in the United States*. Columbus: Ohio State University Press, 2020.

Edelman, Lee. *No Future: Queer Theory and the Death Drive*. Durham, NC: Duke University Press, 2004.

Faludi, Susan. *Stiffed: The Betrayal of the American Man*. Reprint ed. New York: Harper Perennial, 2000.

Fanon, Frantz. *Black Skin, White Masks*. Translated by Richard Philcox. New York: Grove Press, 2008.

Flores, Lisa A. *Deportable and Disposable: Public Rhetoric and the Making of the Illegal Immigrant*. University Park: Pennsylvania State University Press, 2020.

Forchtner, Bernhard. *The Far Right and the Environment: Politics, Discourse and Communication*. New York: Routledge, 2019.

Foucault, Michel. *Discipline and Punish: The Birth of the Prison*. New York: Vintage, 1977.

———. *Security, Territory, Population: Lectures at the Collège de France 1977–1978*. Edited by Michel Senellart. Translated by Graham Burchell. 1st ed. New York: Picador, 2009.

Freud, Sigmund. *Beyond the Pleasure Principle*. New York: International Psycho-Analytical Press, 1922.

Gibson, James William. *Warrior Dreams: Violence and Manhood in Post-Vietnam America*. New York: Hill & Wang, 1994.

Greene, Ronald W. *Malthusian Worlds: U.S. Leadership and the Governing of the Population Crisis*. Boulder, CO: Westview Press, 1999.

Gregg, Melissa, and Gregory J. Seigworth, eds. *The Affect Theory Reader*. Durham, NC: Duke University Press, 2010.

Gunn, Joshua. *Modern Occult Rhetoric: Mass Media and the Drama of Secrecy in the Twentieth Century*. Tuscaloosa: University of Alabama Press, 2005.

———. *Political Perversion: Rhetorical Aberration in the Time of Trumpeteering*. 1st ed. Chicago: University of Chicago Press, 2020.

Hall, Stuart, and Henry Louis Gates Jr. *The Fateful Triangle: Race, Ethnicity, Nation*. Edited by Kobena Mercer. Cambridge, MA: Harvard University Press, 2017.

Hartman, Saidiya V. *Scenes of Subjection: Terror, Slavery, and Self-Making in Nineteenth-Century America*. New York: Oxford University Press, 1997.

Hassan, Riaz. *Life as a Weapon: The Global Rise of Suicide Bombings*. Abingdon, UK: Routledge, 2014.

Hawley, George. *The Alt-Right: What Everyone Needs to Know®*. Oxford University Press, 2018.

———. *Making Sense of the Alt-Right*. New York: Columbia University Press, 2017.

Hinton, Alexander Laban. *It Can Happen Here: White Power and the Rising Threat of Genocide in the US*. New York: New York University Press, 2021.

Hyde, Michael J. *The Call of Conscience* Columbia: University of South Carolina Press, 2001.

Jackson, Ronald L. *Scripting the Black Masculine Body: Identity, Discourse, and Racial Politics in Popular Media*. Albany: SUNY Press, 2006.

Jenkins, Henry. *Convergence Culture: Where Old and New Media Collide*. New York: New York University Press, 2008.

Jenkins, Henry, Sam Ford, and Joshua Green. *Spreadable Media: Creating Value and Meaning in a Networked Culture*. New York: New York University Press, 2013.

Johnson, Paul Elliott. *I, the People: The Rhetoric of Conservative Populism in the United States*. Tuscaloosa: University of Alabama Press, 2021.

Jordan, Winthrop D. *White Over Black: American Attitudes toward the Negro, 1550–1812*. 2nd ed. Chapel Hill: University of North Carolina Press, 2012.

Jowett, Garth S., and Victoria O'Donnell. *Propaganda & Persuasion*. Thousand Oaks, CA: Sage, 2011.

Kaplan, Jeffrey. *Encyclopedia of White Power: A Sourcebook on the Radical Racist Right*. Lanham, MD: Rowman & Littlefield, 2000.

Kellner, Douglas. *Guys and Guns Amok: Domestic Terrorism and School Shootings from the Oklahoma City Bombing to the Virginia Tech Massacre*. Abingdon, UK: Routledge, 2008.

Kelly, Casey R. *Apocalypse Man: The Death Drive and the Rhetoric of White Masculine Victimhood*. Columbus: Ohio State University Press, 2020.

———. *Caught on Tape: White Masculinity and Obscene Enjoyment*. New York: Oxford University Press, 2023.

King, Claire Sisco. *Washed in Blood: Male Sacrifice, Trauma, and the Cinema*. New Brunswick, NJ: Rutgers University Press, 2011.

Kristeva, Julia. *The Power of Horror: An Essay on Abjection*. New York: Columbia University Press, 1982.

Lacan, Jacques. *The Four Fundamental Concepts of Psycho-Analysis*. Norton, 1998.

Lang, Berel. *Genocide: The Act as Idea*. University Park: University of Pennsylvania Press, 2017.

Lechuga, Michael. *Visions of Invasion: Alien Affects, Cinema, and Citizenship in Settler Colonies*. Jackson: University Press of Mississippi, 2023.

Levine, Caroline. *Forms: Whole, Rhythm, Hierarchy, Network*. Princeton, NJ: Princeton University Press, 2015.

Levy, Yael. *Chick TV: Antiheroines and Time Unbound*. Syracuse, NY: Syracuse University Press, 2022.

Loewen, James W. *Sundown Towns: A Hidden Dimension of American Racism*. New York: New Press, 2018.

Lotz, Amanda D. *Cable Guys: Television and Masculinities in the 21st Century*. New York: New York University Press, 2014.

Lundberg, Christian. *Lacan in Public: Psychoanalysis and the Science of Rhetoric*. Tuscaloosa: University of Alabama Press, 2012.

Lyon, Janet. *Manifestoes: Provocations of the Modern*. Ithaca, NY: Cornell University Press, 1999.

Marcuse, Herbert. *The Aesthetic Dimension: Toward a Critique of Marxist Aesthetics*. Boston: Beacon Press, 1978.

Marwick, Alice E. *Status Update: Celebrity, Publicity, and Branding in the Social Media Age*. New Haven, CT: Yale University Press, 2015.

Massumi, Brian. *Parables for the Virtual: Movement, Affect, Sensation*. 1st ed. Durham, NC: Duke University Press Books, 2002.

Mbembe, Achille. *Necropolitics*. Durham, NC: Duke University Press, 2019.

McGowan, Todd. *Enjoying What We Don't Have: The Political Project of Psychoanalysis*. Lincoln: University of Nebraska Press, 2013.

McLeod, Kembrew. *Pranksters: Making Mischief in the Modern World*. New York: New York University Press, 2014.

Melamed, Jodi. *Represent and Destroy: Rationalizing Violence in the New Racial Capitalism*. Minneapolis: University of Minnesota Press, 2011.

Miller-Idriss, Cynthia. *Hate in the Homeland: The New Global Far Right*. Princeton, NJ: Princeton University Press, 2022.

Mills, Charles W. *Black Rights/White Wrongs: The Critique of Racial Liberalism*. New York: Oxford University Press, 2017.

———. *The Racial Contract*. Ithaca, NY: Cornell University Press, 1999.

Mittell, Jason. *Complex TV: The Poetics of Contemporary Television Storytelling*. New York: New York University Press, 2015.

Moore, Sam, and Alex Roberts. *The Rise of Ecofascism: Climate Change and the Far Right*. Wiley, 2022.

Moten, Fred. *Stolen Life*. Durham, NC: Duke University Press, 2018.

Murray, Billie. *Combating Hate: A Framework for Direct Action*. University Park: Pennsylvania State University Press, 2022.

Nagle, Angela. *Kill All Normies: Online Culture Wars from 4Chan and Tumblr to Trump and the Alt-Right*. Winchester, UK; Washington, USA: Zero Books, 2017.

Naimark, Norman M. *Genocide: A World History*. New York: Oxford University Press, 2017.

Neiwert, David. *Alt-America: The Rise of the Radical Right in the Age of Trump*. London: Verso, 2017.

Nickson, Elizabeth. *Eco-Fascists: How Radical Conservationists Are Destroying Our Natural Heritage*. New York: Harper Collins, 2012.

Nilan, Pam. *Young People and the Far Right*. New York: Springer Nature, 2021.

Ore, Ersula J. *Lynching: Violence, Rhetoric, and American Identity*. Jackson: University Press of Mississippi, 2019.

Phillips, Whitney, and Ryan M. Milner. *The Ambivalent Internet: Mischief, Oddity, and Antagonism Online*. Cambridge, UK: Polity Press, 2018.

———. *You Are Here: A Field Guide for Navigating Polarized Speech, Conspiracy Theories, and Our Polluted Media Landscape*. Cambridge, MA: MIT Press, 2021.

Popper, Karl. *The Open Society and Its Enemies*. Abingdon, UK: Routledge, 2012.

Puar, Jasbir K. *The Right to Maim: Debility, Capacity, Disability*. Durham, NC: Duke University Press, 2017.

Quine, Maria-Sophia. *Population Politics in Twentieth Century Europe: Fascist Dictatorships and Liberal Democracies*. Abingdon, UK: Routledge, 2013.

Reich, Wilhelm. *The Mass Psychology of Fascism*. 3rd ed. Translated by Vincent R. Carfagno. New York: Farrar, Straus and Giroux, 1980.

Robinson, Sally. *Authenticity Guaranteed: Masculinity and the Rhetoric of Anti-Consumerism in American Culture*. Amherst, MA: University of Massachusetts Press, 2018.

Rodríguez, Dylan. *White Reconstruction: Domestic Warfare and the Logics of Genocide*. New York: Fordham University Press, 2020.

Salter, Anastasia, and Bridget Blodgett. *Toxic Geek Masculinity in Media: Sexism, Trolling, and Identity Policing*. New York: Palgrave Macmillan, 2017.

Schmid, David. *Natural Born Celebrities: Serial Killers in American Culture*. Chicago: University of Chicago Press, 2006.

Seshadri-Crooks, Kalpana. *Desiring Whiteness: A Lacanian Analysis of Race*. New York: Routledge, 2000.

Sexton, Jared. *Amalgamation Schemes: Antiblackness and the Critique of Multiracialism*. Minneapolis: University of Minnesota Press, 2008.

Slotkin, Richard. *Regeneration Through Violence: The Mythology of the American Frontier, 1600–1860*. Norman: University of Oklahoma Press, 2000.

Spackman, Barbara. *Fascist Virilities: Rhetoric, Ideology, and Social Fantasy in Italy*. Minneapolis: University of Minnesota Press, 1996.

Spiro, Jonathan Peter. *Defending the Master Race: Conservation, Eugenics, and the Legacy of Madison Grant*. Burlington, VT: University of Vermont Press, 2009.

Stern, Alexandra Minna. *Proud Boys and the White Ethnostate: How the Alt-Right Is Warping the American Imagination*. Boston: Beacon Press, 2019.

Strossen, Nadine. *HATE: Why We Should Resist It With Free Speech, Not Censorship*. New York: Oxford University Press, 2018.

Surette, Ray. *Copycat Crime and Copycat Criminals*. Boulder, CO: Lynne Rienner Publishers, 2022.

Taffel, Sy. *Digital Media Ecologies: Entanglements of Content, Code and Hardware*. New York: Bloomsbury, 2019.

Valencia, Sayak. *Gore Capitalism*. Cambridge, MA: MIT Press, 2018.

Warren, Calvin L. *Ontological Terror: Blackness, Nihilism, and Emancipation*. Durham, NC: Duke University Press, 2018.

Weheliye, Alexander G. *Habeas Viscus: Racializing Assemblages, Biopolitics, and Black Feminist Theories of the Human*. Durham, NC: Duke University Press, 2014.

Wilderson, Frank B. *Afropessimism*. New York: Liveright, 2020.

Woods, Heather Suzanne, and Leslie A. Hahner. *Make America Meme Again: The Rhetoric of the Alt-Right*. New York: Peter Lang, 2019.

Žižek, Slavoj. *Looking Awry: An Introduction to Jacques Lacan Through Popular Culture*. Cambridge, MA: MIT Press, 1992.

———. *The Ticklish Subject: The Absent Centre of Political Ontology*. London: Verso, 2000.

———. *Welcome to the Desert of the Real: Five Essays on September 11 and Related Dates*. London: Verso, 2013.

Index